A Manager's Guide to

Improving Workplace Performance

A Manager's Guide to

Improving Workplace Performance

Roger Chevalier

AMACOM
American Management Association
New York • Atlanta • Brussels • Chicago • Mexico City • San Francisco
Shanghai • Tokyo • Toronto • Washington, D.C.

Special discounts on bulk quantities of AMACOM books are available to corporations, professional associations, and other organizations. For details, contact Special Sales Department, AMACOM, a division of American Management Association, 1601 Broadway, New York, NY 10019.
Tel: 212-903-8316. Fax: 212-903-8083.
E-mail: specialsls@amanet.org
Website: www.amacombooks.org/go/specialsales
To view all AMACOM titles go to: www.amacombooks.org

This publication is designed to provide accurate and authoritative information in regard to the subject matter covered. It is sold with the understanding that the publisher is not engaged in rendering legal, accounting, or other professional service. If legal advice or other expert assistance is required, the services of a competent professional person should be sought.

Situational Leadership® is a registered trademark of the Center for Leadership Studies, Inc. For more information, visit www.situational.com.

Library of Congress Cataloging-in-Publication Data

Chevalier, Roger, 1946–
A manager's guide to improving workplace performance / Roger Chevalier.
p. cm.
Includes index.
ISBN-10: 0-8144-7418-7 (pbk.)
ISBN-13: 978-0-8144-7418-1 (pbk.)
1. Personnel management. 2. Employee motivation. 3. Work environment. 4. Employees—Coaching of. I. Title.

HF5549.C4468 2007
658.3'14—dc22 *2006036145*

Printed in the United States of America.

Printing number

10 9 8 7 6 5 4 3 2 1

Contents

Foreword

I had the privilege of serving on the Board of the Peter Drucker Foundation for ten years. Peter continually reinforced the point that management is not an art and management is not a science—management is a practice.

Peter would approve of the fact that Roger Chevalier provides sound advice that managers can actually practice! His tools are both applicable and useful. Instead of being lost in complex theories—which sound good but don't translate into daily behavior—he focuses on sharing applications that managers can immediately put to work. Roger is not just interested in what managers should know—he is interested in what managers can do.

At the end of the day, a manager's job is simple—improving workplace performance. If managers are not improving workplace performance, why are they wasting the organization's valuable resources?

Roger's conclusion at the end of this book says what managers should not forget: "Never lose track of the fact that you create the work environment for your people. They will either excel or flounder based on the work environment that you create with your coaching, leadership, counseling, and team-building skills, as well as the way in which you analyze performance gaps and causes, identify and implement solutions, and measure results."

Along with Peter Drucker, another one of my most important mentors has been Paul Hersey. Ken Blanchard and he developed Situational Leadership® and shared this fantastic model with millions of managers from around the world. Roger is a world leader in understanding and teaching Situational Leadership. *A Manager's*

Guide to Improving Workplace Performance builds upon the teachings of Paul and Ken and provides specific applications that relate to performance management.

I am best known as a leading executive coach. For you, the reader, my coaching is simple—practice using the tools described in this book! Share the ideas with your work team and involve them in your process of planning, coaching, and feedback.

My partner Howard Morgan and I completed an extensive research study on the impact of leadership development involving over eighty-six thousand respondents and eight major corporations.[1] Our findings were very compelling, yet not very surprising. Managers who involved their people back on the job and actually applied the concepts they were taught were seen as becoming far more effective leaders—not by themselves, but by their coworkers. Managers who didn't apply what was learned didn't get any better.

The tools in this book work, but they only work if you apply them. If you involve your people, practice what you learn, and follow up to ensure success, you will be amazed at the results! If you don't *apply* this material it won't help you. Some managers are going to find that this book makes a huge difference in improving workplace performance. Some will say it makes no difference. The change that is ultimately produced from reading this book will not be a reflection on the material. It will be a reflection on you!

Marshall Goldsmith

1. Marshall Goldsmith and Howard Morgan, "Leadership Is a Contact Sport," *Strategy+Business,* Issue 36 (Fall 2004): 71–79.

Acknowledgments

This book could not have been written without the people whom I've supervised, who had to put up with my shortcomings as I learned how to be a manager and coach, the managers I've had as role models, and the instructors who gave me greater insight into what managers should do to be effective.

I have been fortunate to find many good role models and mentors throughout my life. The first was Augie Werkmeister, the owner of the Chicken Delight who provided me with my first manager's role that paid for my college education. Another was Captain Dick Marcott, who guided me in the two assignments during my Coast Guard career when I was head of a leadership school and when I served as a director of training, with a staff of 140 instructors presenting twenty-five courses to 4,000 students a year. And then there was Dick McKenna, who served as my mentor for nearly twenty years as I worked with Century 21 Real Estate as a consultant and finally as a vice president of their Performance Division.

I would be remiss if I didn't mention the three people who shaped my views of leadership and coaching: Paul Hersey, Ken Blanchard, and Marshall Goldsmith. And I add one more colleague, Roger Addison, who has been a mentor for the past five years as I learned more about how to improve workplace performance.

And I owe a special thanks to Adrienne Hickey and Erika Spelman of AMACOM Books for their support and guidance, as well as to April Davis and Mike Lee for the feedback that they provided as I prepared the first draft of this book. I also need to thank Ron Campbell of the Center for Leadership Studies for his support and for the use of the Situational Leadership® Model.

But as much as anyone, I must acknowledge my life partner, Suzanne Chevalier, who guided me in that most important of management roles, the parenting of our children. What I learned through trial and error, and with a lot of study, she did intuitively. I am forever grateful, as are our two sons, that someone in our family knew what she was doing.

A Manager's Guide to Improving Workplace Performance

"If I have seen further it is by standing upon the shoulders of giants."

—SIR ISAAC NEWTON

Introduction

This book is the end product of forty years of preparation that started when I became a manager in a Chicken Delight franchise in Merrick, New York, as I worked my way through college. It was continued with a twenty-year career as an officer in the U.S. Coast Guard, during which I had the opportunity to further develop my managerial skills and to deliver leadership training to both officers and enlisted military personnel.

As part of my development, I had the pleasure to study for six years under Drs. Paul Hersey and Ken Blanchard, the developers of Situational Leadership®, who shaped much of the way I view the manager's role in leading and developing people. It was during this time that I also studied under Dr. Marshall Goldsmith, who added much to my understanding of the manager's role as a coach. I continued to learn as I delivered leadership and coaching training to over 30,000 managers in hundreds of workshops and classes.

From these people and the many mentors who have helped me along the way, I have learned that there is something that underlies all the techniques that are used to improve workplace performance. While this book will provide you with many exceptional tools to improve workplace performance, it also is deeply rooted in a management philosophy of developing people. There is no greater contribution that you will make to the continued success of your organization than that of developing individuals and teams that are better able to respond to the demands of their jobs and the ever-changing work environment.

While much of this book is devoted to developing your employees, it is not about how to "fix" them. Most of the performance problems on the job are caused by the work environment, not the individual employee. So while the book begins with a discussion of your role in developing your people, its real message is that you as a manager are responsible for creating a work environment where your people can succeed.

Performance management provides an overall game plan for interacting with employees. Situational Leadership® addresses another key element: how managers vary the amount of direction and support they give, based on the willingness and ability of their people to do specific tasks. And performance counseling provides the guidelines for giving feedback to an employee. But something was still missing in my description of how managers provide a positive work environment for their people.

I found the pieces I was looking for when I took a full-time position with the International Society for Performance Improvement (ISPI), which had been my professional home for many years. It was there that I was able to identify other aspects of the work environment that contribute to individual and organizational performance. These include such factors as clear expectations, timely feedback, job aids to guide employees, resources (such as time, materials, and equipment), clearly defined processes and procedures, evaluation of activities and results, and incentive systems that reward performance.

For the purpose of this book, I will use the term *manager* to describe anyone who leads and develops others. These roles include traditional organizational positions of managers, first-line supervisors, and shop stewards, as well as nonbusiness roles such as parents and youth sports coaches.

After reading this book, you will be able to:

- Coach your employees through the entire performance period and conduct performance appraisals that will bring about improved on-the-job performance
- Develop your people using Situational Leadership to adjust the amount of direction and support you give based on your employee's willingness and ability to do a given task
- Counsel your people in a way that actually improves performance
- Identify important aspects of individual motivation and teamwork
- Identify performance shortfalls that need to be addressed
- Describe these shortfalls (gaps) in measurable terms
- Identify, weight, and display factors that are working for and against closing the performance gap
- Develop alternative solutions and select the best one
- Implement the necessary changes
- Evaluate the results in terms of impact on a desired business outcome

This book presents a systematic approach for improving workplace performance. It is meant to serve as a practical guide for both managers and human resources professionals. The book is organized into three sections. Section 1 focuses on your role in developing your people and your workgroup. Chapter 1 begins this approach by describing the manager's role as a coach, which begins with a clear communication of expectations by defining activities and results, then observing, providing feedback, recording performance, and adjusting goals throughout the period. This systematic approach ends with getting employee input, reviewing records, and counseling the employee before writing the performance appraisal.

Chapter 2 presents managers as leaders who develop their employees as they assess the ability and willingness of their people, and then provide needed direction and support. Chapter 3 expands these ideas by providing a performance counseling guide that focuses on the coaching and counseling roles that all managers play. Chapter 4 describes what motivates individual employees, and Chapter 5 describes how they work together as a team.

Section 2 focuses on identifying and removing barriers to individual and group performance. Chapter 6 begins an examination of the process used to improve performance by identifying individual and group performance shortfalls as the difference between the present and the desired levels of performance. Chapter 7 provides a structure for systematically analyzing the causes of the performance shortfalls that are related to the work environment as well as the employees. Chapter 8 provides an example of a new team that is not productive. Then the tools described in Chapters 6 and 7 are used to analyze the performance shortfalls and their causes in the case study in Chapter 8.

Chapter 9 offers guidelines for developing alternative strategies and selecting the one with the highest probability of success. The solutions for the case study used in Chapter 8 are then discussed. Chapter 10 presents information on how managers acquire and use the power needed to implement change. Chapter 11 discusses how to evaluate the short- and long-term effects of the change. Chapter 12 provides another example of the performance analysis and change process.

Section 3 brings together all of the ideas on how to create an environment where your people can succeed. Chapter 13 helps you organize all the tools provided in the first twelve chapters in a practical toolbox you can use on the job.

Each chapter concludes with an Application Exercise that you, as a manager, can use with your people. Learning is more than just acquiring knowledge. True learning requires that you apply the new knowledge so that you can realize a real return on your investment—for you, your people, and your organization.

The ideas and models presented in this book will help you to organize what you have already learned from experience so that you can see patterns that led to success or failure and thus better learn from that experience. The structure provided will also allow you to recognize opportunities to improve individual and organizational performance as you create an environment where your people can succeed. The value of what you learn from this book should be measured by the improved performance of your people in producing results that are valued by your organization.

For more information on improving workplace performance and to download larger versions of the application exercises, please visit www.aboutiwp.com.

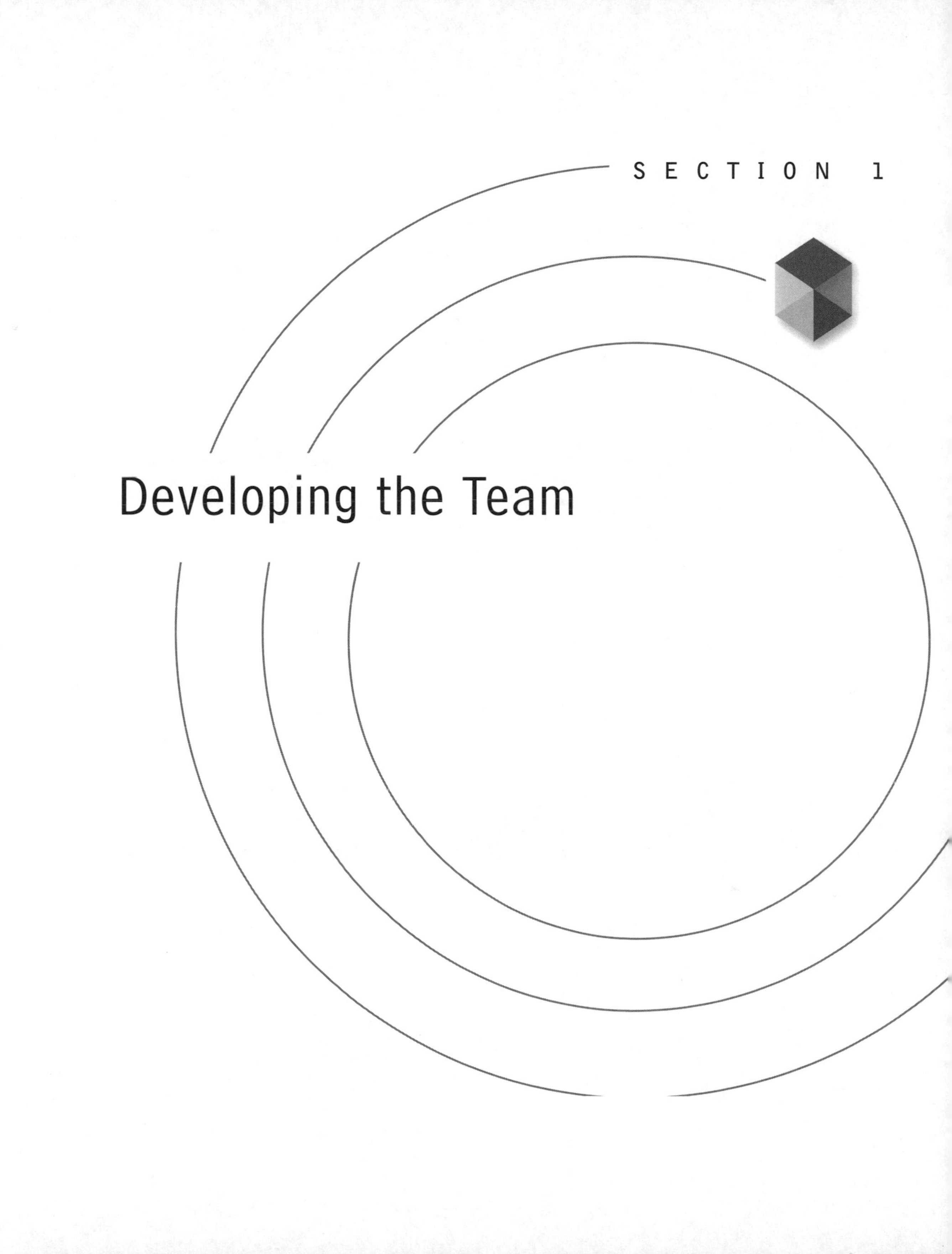

SECTION 1

Developing the Team

> "Efficiency is doing a job right.
> Effectiveness is doing the right job."
>
> —PETER DRUCKER

CHAPTER 1

The Manager as Coach

Here's a message that will either make your day or ruin your year, if you've supervised the same workgroup for more than a year: "You have exactly the employees you deserve." If you have coached your people properly, you should have been able to build a high-performing team within a year. The problem is that many managers have effectively abandoned their team by failing to coach them properly throughout this period.

Your ability to coach people is key to having them do the right job right. Essential to meeting this goal is the way in which you communicate performance expectations and how you coach people throughout the year. Thus, an important role for a manager is that of coach: in this job, you create a positive work environment in which your people can succeed. Performance coaching is the way to do this.

This chapter provides a structure for coaching—for planning, for communicating performance expectations at the beginning of the period, observing performance, and providing feedback, as well as for conducting a performance review at the end of the period.[1]

The Performance-Coaching Process

How long has it been since you performed a formal performance evaluation for your team members? For many employees it has been years since their manager took the time to provide feedback via a formal performance-counseling session. Even for employees who do receive regular reviews, this counseling session is probably not the highlight of their year.

For example, in many organizations, the performance-coaching process has been reduced to a once-a-year appraisal session that can best be described as an "end-of-period autopsy"—a meeting to determine what went wrong. Very often, managers become judge and jury, limiting their ability to truly improve the performance of their people. As such, performance management becomes an annual intervention rather than a continuous process. The manager's efforts are limited to meeting organizational needs for information from the appraisal with which to make administrative decisions on promotions, terminations, pay raises, bonuses, and training. But what about the needs of the employees for clearly communicated expectations and timely feedback on performance? And how accurate will the annual appraisal be if performance records are not kept throughout the year?

Developing a Plan

The process of coaching begins with having an overall plan for your workgroup that aligns with the organization's goals for the same period. Without a plan you will not know how to coach your people. There's a part of Lewis Carroll's *Alice in Wonderland* that applies here.[2] Alice has no idea where she is or where she is going when the path she is following comes to a fork, where she can go one of two ways. She needs to make a decision which way to go, when suddenly the Cheshire Cat appears in the tree where the path divides.

"Cheshire Puss," she began, "Would you tell me, please, which way I ought to go from here?"

"That depends a good deal on where you want to get to," said the Cat.

"I don't much care where—" said Alice.

"Then it doesn't matter which way you go," said the Cat.

It's not enough for you to take your employees "somewhere"; it *does* matter which path they take. As a manager you must have a clear vision of where you and your people are going and how you will get there. But this requires a bit of planning on your part, and there are many excuses managers give for not planning. These excuses include:

- No time for planning
- Short-range demands dominate
- Rewards for short-term performance only
- Overly optimistic or pessimistic viewpoint
- Uncertain work environment
- Rapidly changing roles and job demands
- Complacency
- Fear of failure or fear of success
- No greater organizational plan
- Those who plan ahead get to do it twice

While a list of reasons for not planning can go on and on, there are also many reasons why you should plan ahead. Doing so:

- Affords greater alignment with organizational goals
- Focuses your efforts as well as those of your employees
- Captures the motivation of your people
- Provides longer lead times for projects
- Helps you cope with changes in key personnel
- Produces measurable results
- Is useful in gathering outside support for projects
- Provides means for competing for resources needed to execute your plan

- Capitalizes on chance occurrences
- Makes things happen

What is it that you really want your team to accomplish during this week, this month, this quarter, this year? Is it aligned with your organization's goals for the same period? How will you measure the results? Can the results be measured in terms of quality, quantity, time, and cost? Always begin every project with its end in mind.

Setting SMART Goals

To begin, you need to establish SMART goals for your workgroup. The acronym SMART stands for *S*pecific; *M*easurable in terms of quality, quantity, time, and cost; *A*ccepted by your people; *R*ealistic to achieve; and *T*ime-bound in that there is a deadline for completion. To be accepted by your people, the SMART goals should be both challenging and achievable. While performance goals may be set by your organizations, you want your employees to help plan how those goals will be accomplished.

The process you should follow in SMART planning for your workgroup is:

1. Review organizational goals to see what measurable results are expected for your workgroup.
2. Develop results for the workgroup in terms of quality, quantity, time, and costs that will measure the effectiveness and efficiency of how you deliver products and/or services.
3. Share these goals with your people and discuss how they can be achieved.
4. Develop a plan that describes the activities needed to meet the goals and achieve the desired outcomes, with measures for quality, quantity, time, and cost.
5. Establish priorities for competing activities and goals.
6. Set milestones (dates and measurable outcomes) to track progress toward reaching the goals.

Beginning the Performance-Appraisal Period

Once you have an overall plan in place, your next step in the performance-coaching process is to interact with direct reports in three distinct phases: preparation, coaching, and review. At the beginning of the performance-appraisal cycle, as depicted in Figure 1-1, you need to clearly define your overall expectations for employee performance during the period. You identify and discuss both the means (tasks/activities) and the ends (outcomes/results) in terms of the performance standards that have been set.

In many organizations, there is no real beginning to the year-long performance-evaluation period, not much happens during this period, and there is little or no constructive feedback at the end. As mentioned earlier, often the comments given and the scores received in the end-of-period appraisal come as a surprise to the employees, and events that have occurred near the end of this period frequently have a greater impact on the appraisal than do those at the beginning.

If you have not clearly communicated your expectations to employees regarding both their key activities and the desired results; if you haven't taken the time to observe your employees and provide timely, behaviorally specific feedback; if you haven't kept records of your employees' performance throughout the appraisal period; if you haven't gotten their input and held a constructive counseling session; then you haven't earned the right to write their evaluations.

A manager needs to begin the appraisal period by reviewing the plans for the workgroup and identifying what each employee must do to be successful. For new or poorly performing employees, you need to communicate your expectations clearly, in terms of the activities they need to do to succeed (such as learning specific skills, working as a team player, or treating customers with respect), as well as the results that should ensue (such as projects to be completed, reports to be submitted, or specific goals to be met).

For experienced and successful employees, you need to focus primarily on the desired results, allowing these experienced employees to help define the activities needed to accomplish the goals and, if possible, assist in setting the goals.

FIGURE 1-1. BEGINNING THE PERFORMANCE-COACHING PROCESS

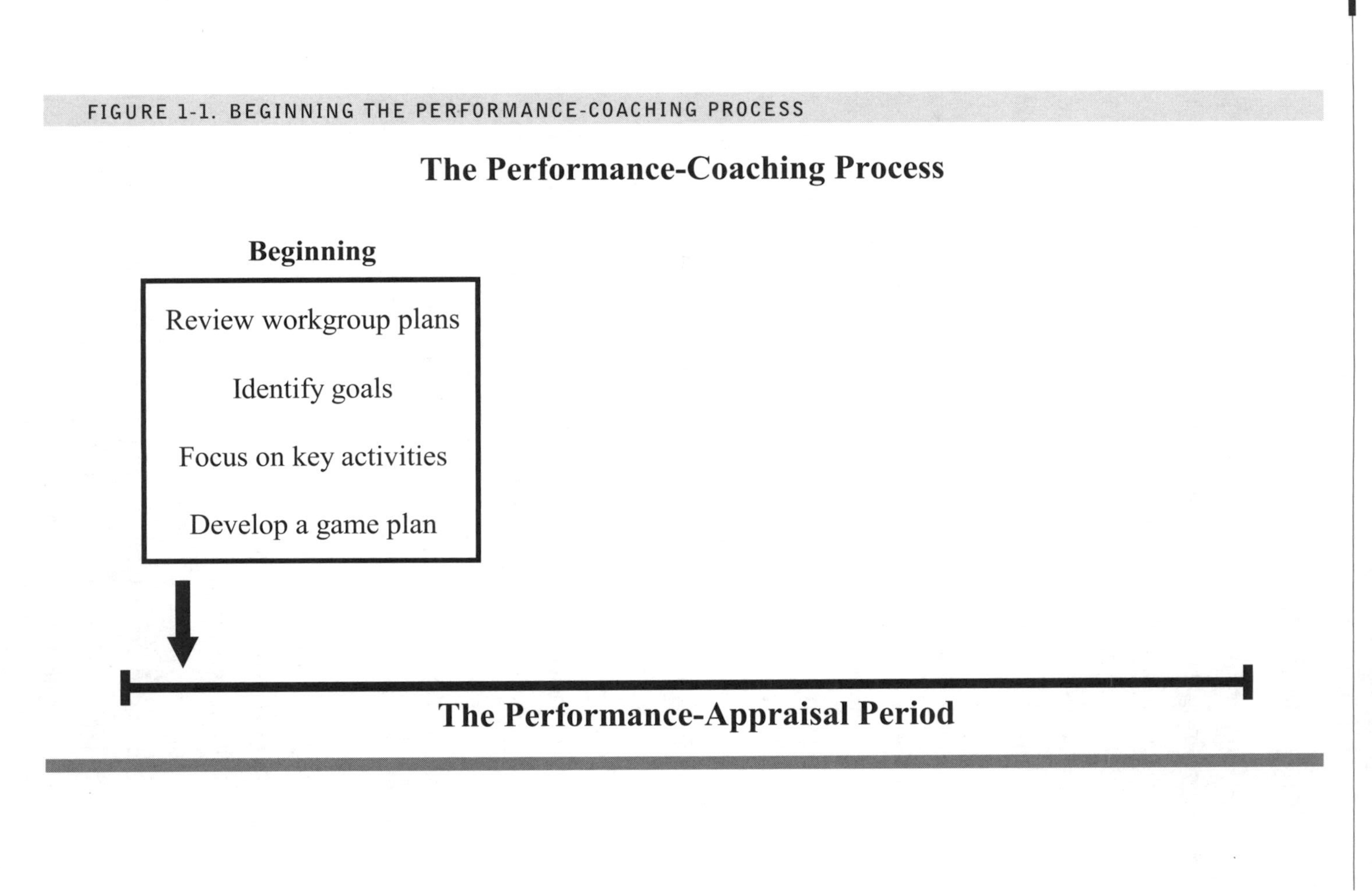

During the Performance-Appraisal Period

Figure 1-2 shows the actions that take place during the appraisal cycle. This is the period when you manage the performance of your workgroup. You directly observe your employees' performance, get feedback from others who have contact with the individuals, and review their productivity against the goals. You provide timely feedback to each employee on his or her performance, adjusting the individual's activities and goals as necessary. Your feedback always focuses on the individual's performance, reinforcing what the person is doing right as well as identifying what needs to be improved.

Throughout the performance-appraisal period, you should also adjust goals as necessary and review activities to ensure that they are contributing to accomplishment of the goal. Since most managers have many people reporting directly to them, and since the performance-appraisal cycle can be as long as a year, it is important to keep written files that document the performance of each employee. And you must keep those records in the same way for all your employees.

For instance, a common mistake that managers make is to keep extensive records only on poor performers. This is called "keeping book" on employees. If a decision is made to terminate the individual, and that person goes to court, you will need to show your records on all the other employees you supervise as evidence that you treat all of your employees the same way. Failure to do so could lead to the court finding fault with the way in which the employee was terminated.

When to Give Feedback

As mentioned at the beginning of the chapter, feedback is a critical part of the performance-coaching process. Once you've clearly communicated your expectations to your employees, you must take the time to observe their work and provide timely feedback on their performance.

There are two types of feedback that you should provide your employees.[3] The first is *motivational*, which you should give as soon as possible after the employee has performed a task, thereby encouraging and supporting the person. The second

FIGURE 1-2. DURING THE PERFORMANCE-COACHING PROCESS

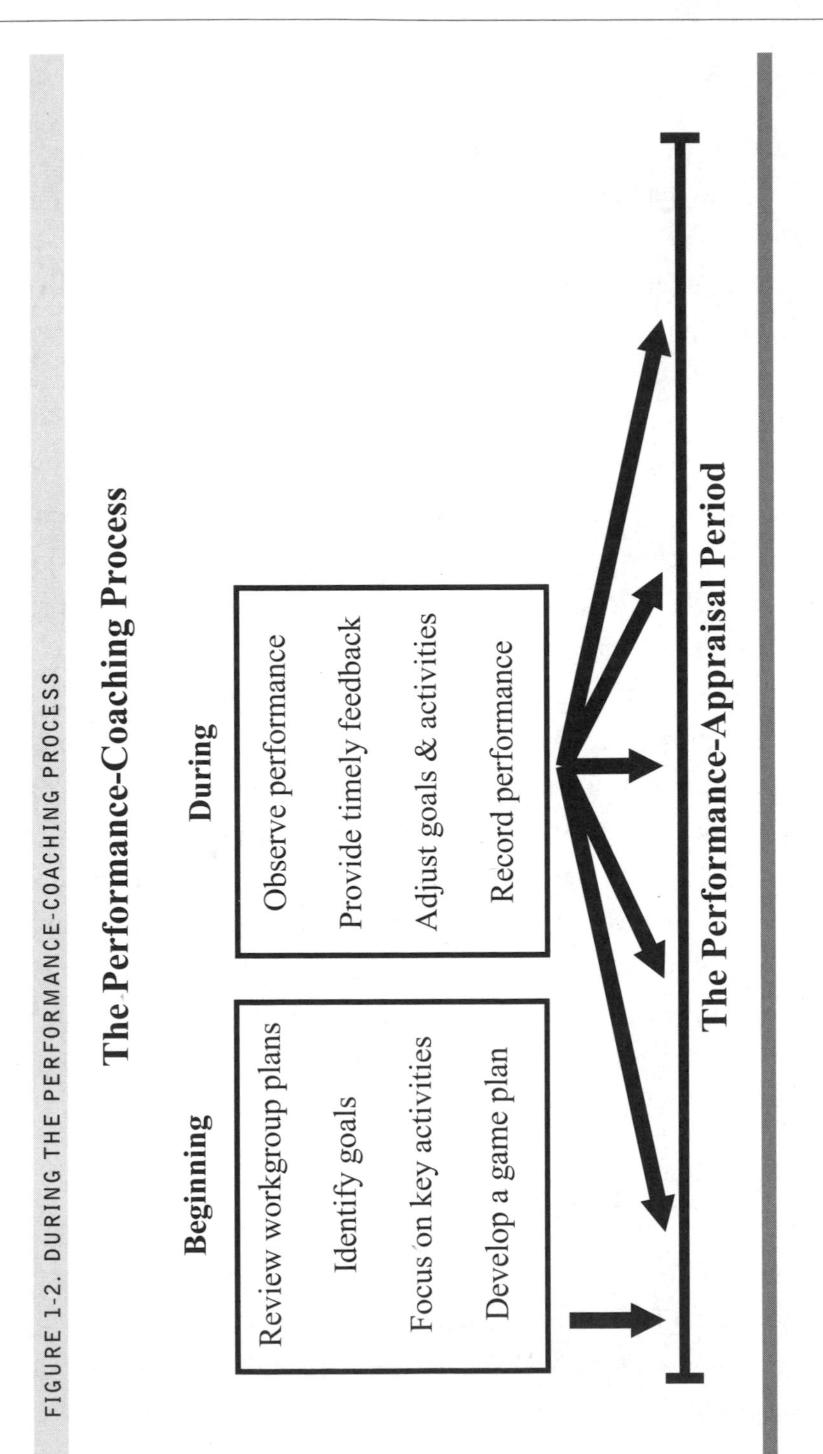

is *corrective*, which you should give just before the person does the task again; this allows your employee to use the feedback as soon as it is given. Sometimes motivational and corrective feedback can be given together, such as when the task will be repeated right away; other times they should be separated, as when the employee will not perform the task for a while.

As an example of coaching, let's consider youth soccer. When the players are on the field, all a coach can do is shout encouragement to the youngsters. The right time for that coach to instruct or provide corrective feedback is just before he or she sends a player into the game as a substitute. This allows players to use what the coach has told them as soon as they enter the game. Too many youth sports coaches, and too many managers, give corrective feedback when they should be giving motivational feedback.

Giving Quality Feedback

Most people enjoy participating in sports because of the clarity of the goals and the amount of feedback they are given on performance. If you bowl in a league, the *goals* are clear: you need to bowl at your average or better. Ideally, you should bowl a perfect game, but more realistically, you look to improve your average. You receive *feedback* from the way the ball feels in your hands, your approach to the line, the way the ball is released, the path the ball takes, the number of pins that you knock down, and the score that's projected above your head.

If we turn this into a typical work example, you'd have the manager half-way down the alley holding a big curtain so that you couldn't see the pins. You'd roll the ball down the alley though the curtain and hear the crash of the pins. The manager would then yell to you, "You missed three." With that type of vague feedback, you'd take your best shot again not knowing where the three missed pins are. The next thing you'd hear is the sound of the ball hitting the back cushion after missing the remaining pins. How long do you think you'd want to continue bowling this way?

A manager's feedback should be specific, focusing on exactly what the employee did that was important. It is not enough to say, "Great job!"—since the employee will not know what is being reinforced. You need to identify *exactly* what it was that the employee did and why it was important. For example, "Mary, I really appreciate the way you dealt with the customers you just helped. By taking the extra time to explain why interest rates are rising, you allowed them to make a better decision as to which loan met their needs in the long run."

Feedback also needs to be balanced. Remember the 4-to-1 rule. For an employee to believe he or she is being treated fairly, the ratio of positive motivational feedback to corrective feedback should be four to one. To use Ken Blanchard's line from *The One Minute Manager*, "Catch your people doing something right."[4] Too many managers provide feedback only when something goes wrong. This is called "management by exception": a manager focuses on negative performance by giving only corrective feedback. If you want to create a positive work environment, provide motivational feedback whenever your employees perform well, and then your corrective feedback will be well received when given.

Ending the Performance-Appraisal Period

This final stage of the performance-appraisal period (see Figure 1-3) is the time to provide feedback in a counseling session that closes out the cycle and begins the next appraisal period. Have each employee submit a written self-evaluation that identifies both accomplishments and shortcomings; this forces the employees to assess their own performance while it also provides you with insights into how each person sees his or her performance.

You should review all performance results, comparing the employee's accomplishments to the goals, along with your records of direct observations and feedback from other sources. You are then ready to counsel the employees prior to completing the annual performance appraisals. Counseling them before writing their appraisals allows you to view "the other side of the story" prior to making your final assessments.

FIGURE 1-3. ENDING THE PERFORMANCE-COACHING PROCESS

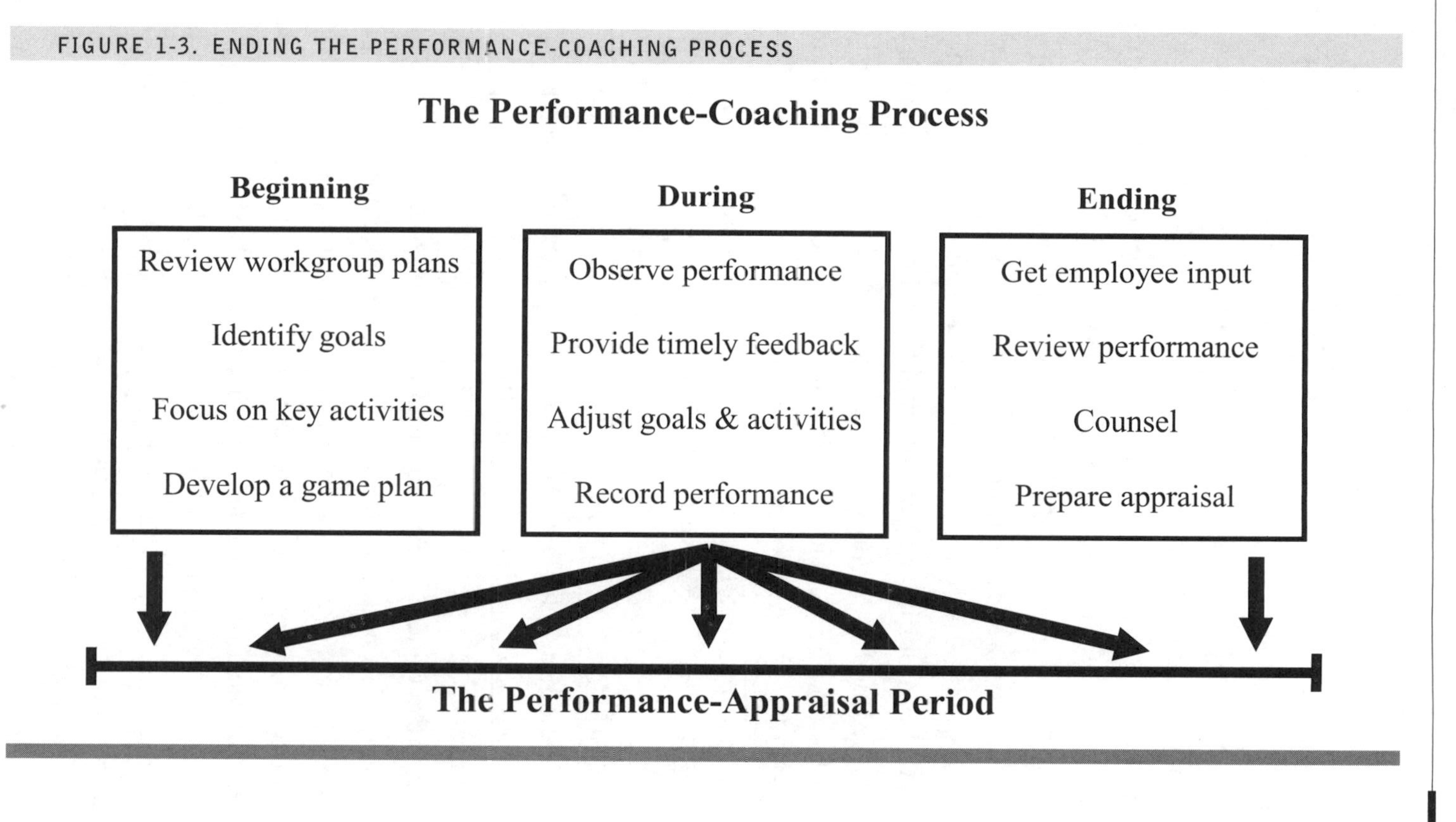

The Elements of Coaching

Of the various behaviors involved in coaching employees, communicating your expectations and providing timely, specific feedback are the most critical. An execise that I have done with a number of organizations is to ask managers to list the five most important tasks each of their employees must do to be successful. Then I ask those employees to list the five most important things they must do to be successful. Very often, only two of the five listed items match, which illustrates the gap between the managers' expectations and those of their employees. These gaps are often documented as unsatisfactory performance in the annual performance appraisal.

Many employees only learn at the end of their performance period what they should have been doing from the beginning. This situation reminds me of a story told by the comedian George Carlin, who is known for his use of "four-letter words" in his routines. Carlin relates how his mother hit him when he said his first swear word. George asked, "What was that for?"

"That was for saying that word; don't ever say it again," his mother responded.

George then asked, "What other words can't I say?"

His mother responded, "I won't tell you, but you'll get hit again when you say one." Unfortunately, that's how many employees learn their jobs—by being "hit in the back of the head" for not doing what they didn't know they should do or by having a year's worth of not-meeting-the-manager's-expectations documented in an annual appraisal.

I learned the value of clearly communicating one's expectations as a youth sports coach, having coached over forty baseball, soccer, indoor soccer, and wrestling teams. What became very apparent was that I needed to communicate my expectations to both the players *and* their parents at a team meeting before the season began. At this meeting, I defined my role, my coaches' roles, the players' roles, and the parents' roles. I avoided a lot of problems by making sure that everyone was aware of his or her role. For example, I told the parents that their job was to cheer at the games, not coach. I explained to them that there would be times when they wouldn't know why their son was not doing what they expected because he was doing what *I* expected. To this I added a game-related example: We are behind by two runs, and their son is at the plate. I give him the sign to take the first pitch to try to get on with a walk. He meets my expectation and does not swing at a pitch that was right in the center of the strike zone. Parents who think they are coaches in the stands may yell, "Get that bat off your shoulder," thinking their son or daughter just let a great pitch go by. This extra "coaching" can be frustrating and confusing to a player who is trying to meet the coach's expectations.

Tips on Performance Coaching

The following are some tips gleaned from years of coaching:

- Start the coaching process with a review of organizational goals. If they don't exist, you will have to develop them yourself. Employees should know how their work contributes to organizational goals. It is your responsibility to make this link for them.
- The position description may be a good starting point for your discussion of the employee's activities, but many of these descriptions are out of date and do not reflect what the employee actually will do. Most position descriptions are limited to activities and do not express the expected results. Your employees will need to have up-to-date information on both activities and results if the performance-coaching process is to be effective.
- Allow your employees to give their input on what activities and results are important. Make sure that you have reached agreement as to what is important. Good performance coaching starts with this agreement. Set performance goals that are both challenging and realistic; goals that are set too high will not motivate your employees.
- Observe performance and provide specific feedback on performance frequently throughout the performance-appraisal period. Nothing should come as a surprise to your employees when you hold the formal counseling session just before writing the appraisal.

- Work to develop your employees in every interaction. Give positive feedback as soon as possible after they perform well, and corrective feedback just before they do the task again.
- Confront poor performance when it happens or as soon afterward as possible. When your poor performers are held accountable, good performers will feel rewarded.
- Learn to ask what happened rather than assuming the worst. (There will be more on questioning techniques in Chapter 3.)
- At the end of the performance period, ask employees for input on their performance. At a minimum, ask employees to list the five most important things they do to be successful, the five most important accomplishments they had during the period, and what they are doing to improve themselves.
- Have a file for each of your employees in which copies of memos and letters that comment on performance can be placed with short notes that record the date and the exceptional performance (either positive or negative) and the feedback provided. Update employee records at least once a week.
- Always hold the formal counseling session before writing the appraisal. You will have your employees' attention when you tell them that this is the last meeting you will have with them before you write the appraisal. You will also be more open to what the employee has to say if you haven't already committed to an evaluation. (You will learn about how to hold this formal counseling session in Chapter 3.)
- "Catch your people doing something right." These words from Ken Blanchard, author of the *One Minute Manager* books, are worth repeating. You should look for and reinforce positive work and not lie back and wait for something to go wrong. If you consistently reinforce poor performance, your employees will give you more poor performance. Make them feel like they have the opportunity to succeed every day.
- Praise in public and criticize in private, but be sensitive to employees who are uncomfortable being praised in front of their peers.

APPLICATION EXERCISE

To transfer what you've just read to your role as a manager in your workplace you will find the following exercise helpful.

For each of the people you supervise, list the five most important *tasks* (activities) that they must do to be successful. Then write down the five most important *results* they must achieve. Have each employee do the same exercise, writing down the five most important tasks and five most important results that they need to achieve to be successful on the job. Use Figure 1-4 to complete this exercise. (For a larger version of this and the other application exercise forms, visit www.aboutiwp.com.)

After each of your employees has completed the lists, discuss the differences between what you have written and what they have written. The result of this discussion should be a list of activities and results that you both agree are necessary for them to be successful on the job.

Notes

1. Paul Hersey and Roger Chevalier, "Situational Leadership and Performance Coaching," in *Coaching for Leadership,* eds. Marshall Goldsmith, Laurence Lyons, and Alyssa Freas (San Francisco: Jossey-Bass Pfeifer, 2000).
2. Lewis Carroll, *Alice's Adventures in Wonderland* (New York: Signet Classics, 2000).
3. Donald Tosti and Stephanie Jackson, "Feedback," *Handbook of Performance Technology,* 2nd ed. (San Francisco: Jossey-Bass Pfeifer, 1999).
4. Kenneth Blanchard and Spencer Johnson, *The One Minute Manager* (New York: William Morrow & Co., 1982).

FIGURE 1-4. ACTIVITIES AND RESULTS EXERCISE

Name: ______________________________

List the five most important tasks (activities) needed to be done to be successful on the job:

1. ______________________________
____

2. ______________________________
____

3. ______________________________
____

4. ______________________________
____

5. ______________________________
____

Now list the five most important results needed to be successful on the job:

1. ______________________________
____

2. ______________________________
____

3. ______________________________
____

4. ______________________________
____

5. ______________________________
____

> **"Pull the string, and it will follow wherever you wish. Push it, and it will go nowhere at all."**
>
> —DWIGHT D. EISENHOWER

CHAPTER 2

The Manager as Leader

You may have encountered a situation where you did not complete a project on time because of other demands. Your boss came into your work area and began to hammer you with a lot of directions, telling you what you should have done, when you should have done it, and where it should have been done, and reminding you that you were responsible for getting it done. How did you feel?

A more appropriate intervention for your boss to take might have been to ask you an open-ended question such as, "Can you tell me what happened that caused you to be late with the project?" With a role model like that manager, you would know how to handle the same situation with your own employees or possibly with your children. That's because good leadership creates a positive work environment that breeds success.

A critical aspect of your role as a manager is to adjust your leadership style to meet the ability and willingness of your people. As a manager you have probably already learned that you need to adjust your leadership style to match an employee's ability to get the job done. For example, if the employee does not know how to do a given task, you need to supply direction, telling the employee what to do, when to do it, how and where to do it, and whom else to involve. If the employee knows how to do a given task, you don't need to give as much direction.

But what about the employee's motivation to do the job? Does the employee want to do the job? Is that employee confident or does he or she need psychological support in order to get the job done? There's no one leadership style for every employee or for every task to be done. You need to adjust the amount of direction and support to match the needs of each employee if you are going to be successful as a leader.

This chapter will focus on how you can use leadership to develop your employees as individuals and as a team. Your role as a leader is a key element in the way in which you create an environment where your people can succeed and where you improve workplace performance.

Becoming a Manager

Remember how easy it used to be when you just had to do the job? You knew what needed to be done, and you did it.

It was just you and the task to be done. And because you were so good at doing that job, you were promoted to a management position so that you could ensure that others would do the job as well as you did. But being a manager is a very different role, requiring skills very different from accomplishing a specific task. Indeed, the degree of difficulty has gone up, as you work through others to get the same job done.

How many times have you thought, as you attempted to guide one of your employees to do a job, "It would be easier to do it myself"? The most fundamental definition of *leadership* is *working through others to get a task done*. You are no longer judged by how well you can do the task you used to do. You are now judged on how well you can get others to do it. You must adopt a leadership role and guide others.

Before you can choose an appropriate leadership style, you need to assess the readiness of your employees to do the specific tasks for which they are responsible. Ultimately you will need to adjust your leadership style to fit the people you are working through. You will need to vary the amount of direction and support you give them, based on their ability and willingness to do the given tasks.

As a leader, you must be flexible, as there is no "best way" that is right for all your employees all the time. While many believe that a leader must be consistent, your consistency must be in how well you match your leadership style to the ability and willingness of your people. To do otherwise is to confuse your employees and treat them unfairly.

Follower Readiness

The key to selecting an appropriate leadership style is found in the follower's readiness (ability and willingness) to do a specific task. *Ability* is defined as the employee's knowledge, experience, and skills needed to do a specific task. *Willingness* is the employee's desire and confidence to do a given task. The follower's readiness can be described on a scale from low to high, with Readiness Level 1 (R1) being the lowest and Readiness Level 4 (R4) being the highest level of readiness to do a specific task. Figure 2-1 shows the four levels of readiness.

- *Readiness Level 1*: The lowest readiness level is that of being unable and unwilling or insecure. Employees who are new or who have been given new tasks may lack the knowledge, experience, and skills to do the task. They may also be unwilling to do the task because they lack desire or confidence.

- *Readiness Level 2*: New employees may begin at a higher readiness level even though they are unable to do a new task because they have the desire to do the task or have confidence in their ability to learn the task. Managers should treat these individuals differently from those who lack desire and/or confidence.

- *Readiness Level 3*: As employees learn a new task they become apprehensive when they begin to do the task on their own. Employees may also regress to this readiness level from being able and willing. Either way, employees at the R3 level are able to do the task but are unwilling or insecure.

- *Readiness level 4*: This is the highest readiness level, when employees are able, willing, and confident to do a given task. They are experienced at doing the specific task and confident in their ability to do it.

FIGURE 2-1. EMPLOYEE READINESS LEVELS

High	Moderate		Low
Able, willing & confident **R4**	Able but unwilling or insecure **R3**	Unable but willing or confident **R2**	Unable & unwilling or insecure **R1**

There are only three ways to have R4 employees. The first is to hire them at that level. This can be expensive, since you are effectively buying these individuals in the employment marketplace. The advantage is that they are fully trained and ready to be productive the day they arrive. The disadvantage is that they don't know your ways of doing business and may not fit in with your other employees.

The second way is to develop R4 employees yourself. You hire them at the R1 and R2 levels and then train and develop them. Developing them yourself will give you more integrated members on your team who tend to be more loyal, since they owe their development to you. If your people develop because of you, they will tend to stay. If they don't develop, or if they develop despite you, they will be terminated or leave on their own. This is why you have exactly the people you deserve. The main disadvantage of developing new employees is the time and energy it takes to develop these people.

The third way is the most common, as observed in my work with a variety of clients. This is prayer. New employees are hired at the R1 and R2 levels, and everyone prays that they don't "screw up" too badly before they learn their jobs. This is the most popular and the most risky way, but there is a way around this problem.

Building a Model for Leadership

Leadership is the amount of task behavior (*direction*) and relationship behavior (*support*) that you give employees as their manager. Direction is when you tell employees what to do, how to do it, when to do it, where to do it, and whom else to do it with. Support is when you engage in two-way communications, actively listen to your employees, provide feedback and encouragement, and use recognition to reinforce the employee's efforts.

You should use high amounts of task behavior when the employee lacks the ability to do the job, but you should reduce the amount of direction as the employee learns what to do. Similarly, you should vary the amount of relationship behavior you provide to take into account your employee's willingness, or the amount of desire and confidence that the employee has to do a specific task. This change in manager behavior varies from high to low involvement, with the range of possible leadership styles as combinations of direction and support. These ranges are shown in Figure 2-2.

Figure 2-3 represents all of the possible leadership styles that occur as the amounts of task and relationship behavior are varied. Every point inside the box is a different leadership style.

Figure 2-4 is a matrix whose axes represent the high and low amounts of direction and support that a manager can exert. The two intersecting lines represent the

(text continued on page 31)

FIGURE 2-2. LEADER BEHAVIORS

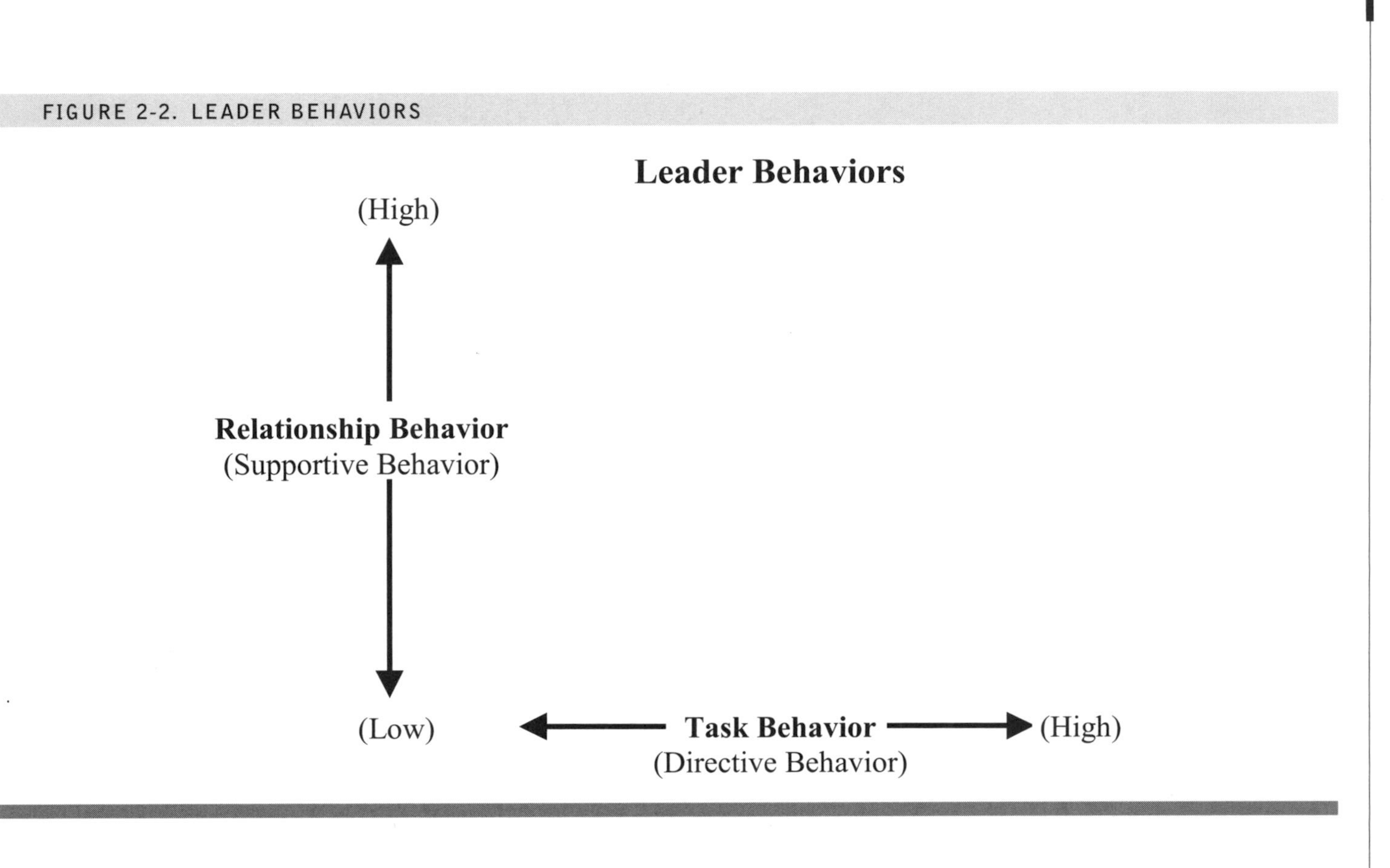

FIGURE 2-3. LEADERSHIP POSSIBILITIES

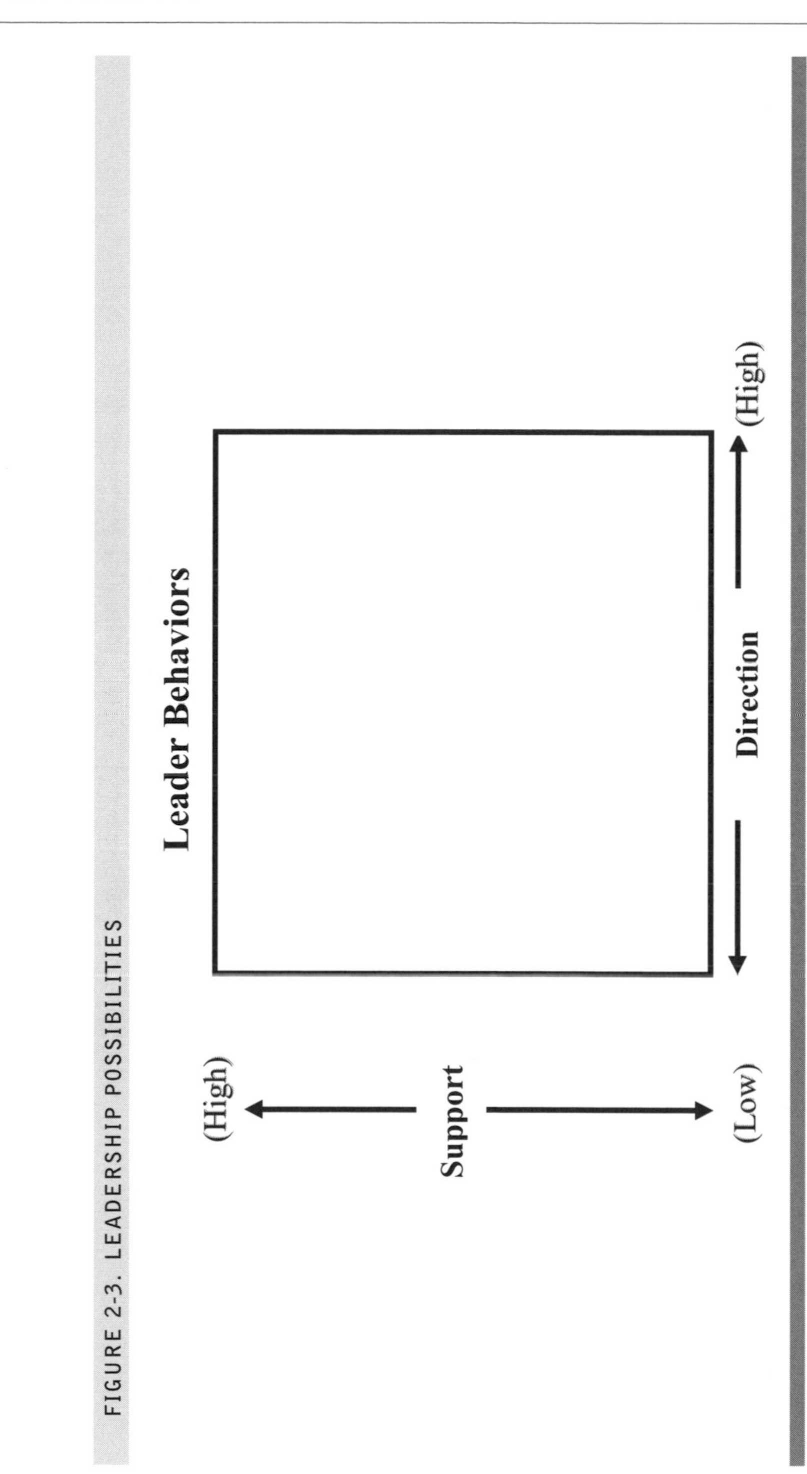

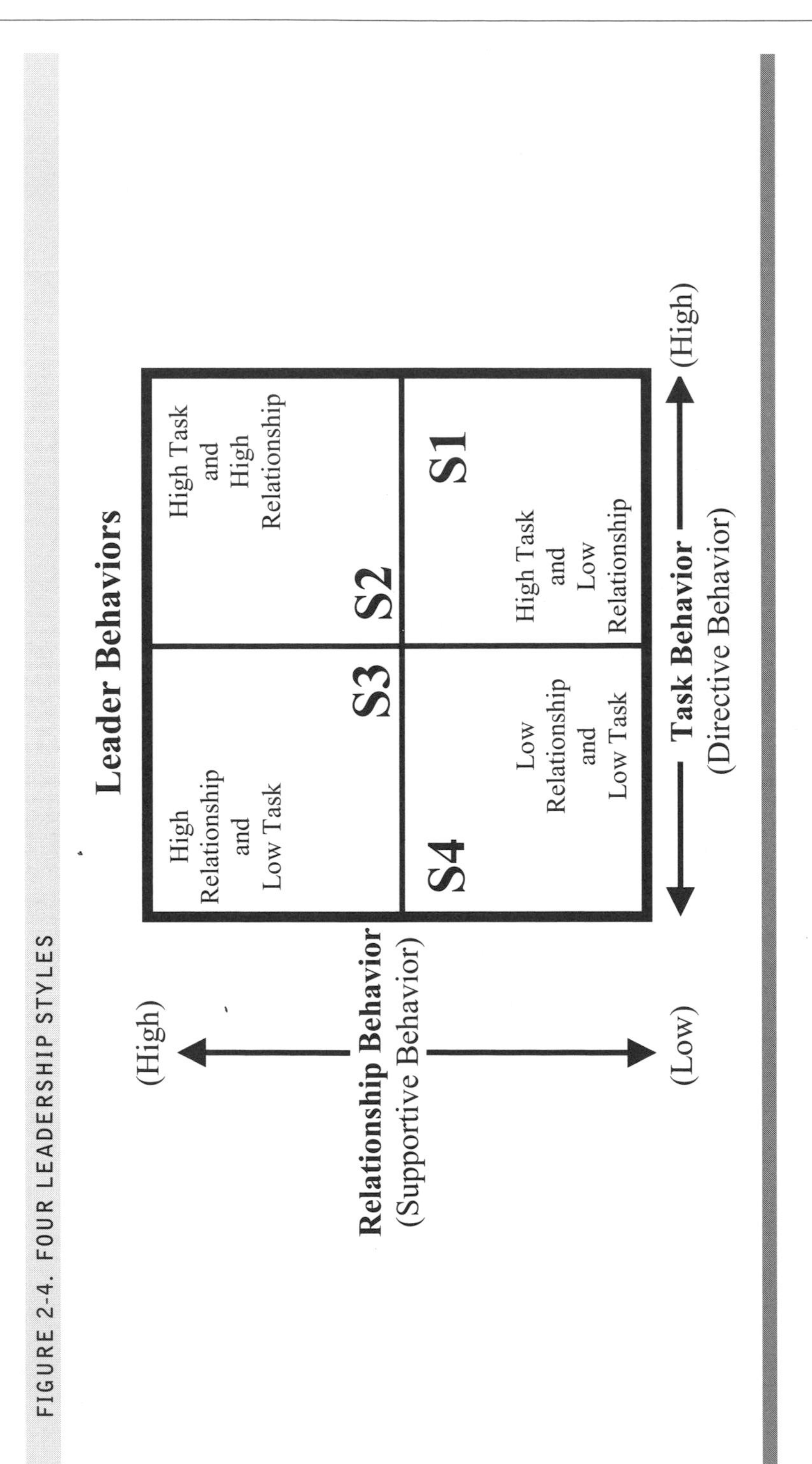

FIGURE 2-4. FOUR LEADERSHIP STYLES

average amounts of direction and support that leaders use. Four basic leadership types appear: high direction/low support; high direction/high support; high support/low direction; and low direction/low support. As a manager, you can use any of these styles by varying the amount of direction and support that you give to your people.

The Situational Leadership® Model

The Situational Leadership Model, developed by Paul Hersey and Ken Blanchard, is used by well over 10 million managers and leaders worldwide.[1] The underlying principle for the model is that managers adjust their leadership styles to accommodate the readiness level (ability and willingness) of their employees to perform each task. Figure 2-5 shows the Situational Leadership Model, with its matrix showing how leaders adjust their leadership styles to take into account the readiness of their followers.

The lowest readiness level (R1) calls for a Style 1 (S1) leadership style, that of providing high amounts of task behavior (direction), since the follower is not able, and low amounts of relationship behavior (support), since the leader does not want to reinforce the follower's unwillingness. The next readiness level (R2) calls for a Style 2 (S2) leadership style, providing high amounts of both task and relationship behavior. Since the employee is still not able but is willing, the leader gives high amounts of task behavior to guide the work being done and high amounts of relationship behavior to reinforce the follower's willingness. The leader works closely with the employee to learn what it will take to be successful—the leader still communicates job expectations and direction but engages in two-way communications rather than just telling the employee what to do.

For the next readiness level (R3), the appropriate leadership style is Style 3 (S3), that of giving high amounts of relationship behavior to build employee confidence and low amounts of task behavior, since the follower is able to do the task. As these employees develop, they typically become apprehensive about how they will do on

FIGURE 2-5. THE SITUATIONAL LEADERSHIP® MODEL

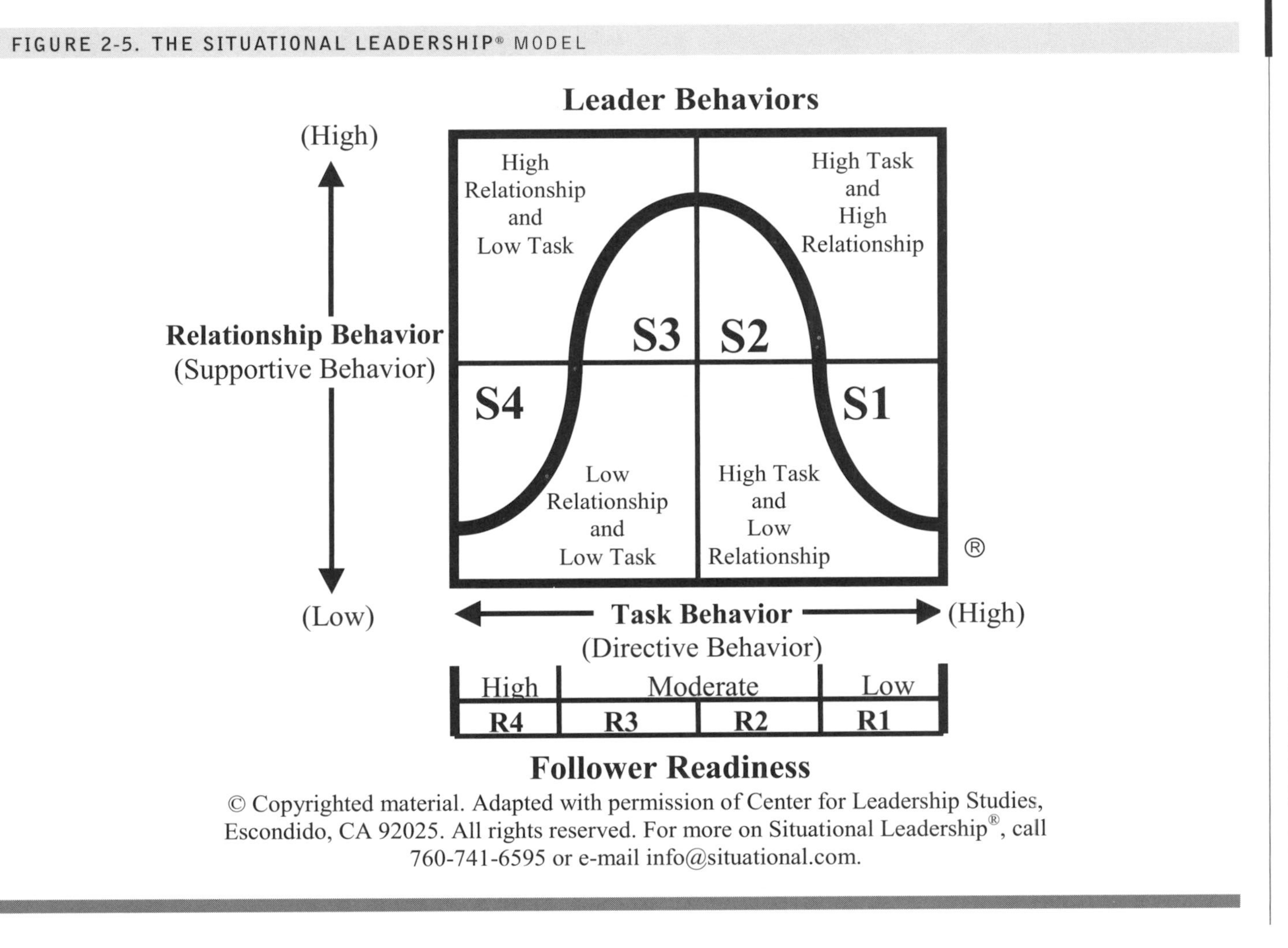

their own, so the Style 3 approach supports them as they begin to work more independently.

The highest readiness level is R4, and the appropriate leadership style is Style 4 (S4), that of giving low amounts of task and relationship behavior since the follower is now both willing and able to do the task. Remember that proper use of Style 4 is that of delegation, not abdication—that Style 4 has *low* amounts of direction and support, not *no* amounts.

The Situational Leadership Model provides a framework for diagnosing different situations, and it prescribes which leadership style will have the highest probability of success in each situation. Using the model will make you more effective as a manager, in that it illustrates the connection between your choice of leadership style and the readiness of your employees. The Situational Leadership Model is a powerful tool in the performance-coaching process.

Using the Situational Leadership Model

The starting point for using the Situational Leadership Model is to identify the key tasks or activities that your employees must do to be successful.[2] You then assess each employee's readiness level for each of the tasks. Then you select the appropriate leadership style. This can be done by observing the employee's performance (Style 4), asking the employee open-ended questions regarding performance (Style 3), and then asking more direct questions (Style 2), if necessary. This assessment technique will be developed further in Chapter 3.

If you believe that the employee is unable and unwilling or insecure in doing the task, intervene with a Style 1 by clearly communicating your expectations and provide direction as to how to improve performance. If you believe that the employee is unable but is willing to learn or is confident, intervene with a Style 2, discussing your expectations as well as being supportive of the employee's willingness to learn.

If you believe that the employee is able to do the task but is unwilling or insecure, be supportive by actively listening to the employee's concerns and recognizing the ability to do the task. If you believe that the follower is able, willing, and confident, allow freedom to perform the task with little direction or support from you.

The Leadership Model in Action

The principles behind the Situational Leadership Model can become institutionalized in an organization, with positive results. For example, during my career in the U.S. Coast Guard, I was to be broken in as an underway Officer of the Deck (OD). But after having spent three years in a shore assignment, I had forgotten a lot of what I had learned about seamanship from my days as an officer candidate. Needless to say, I was unable to walk on board a 378-foot Coast Guard cutter and get her underway. I was also a bit apprehensive about the responsibilities I would be assuming, which included the safety of the 165 men who would sail with me.

The breaking-in process began with a Style 1 leadership mode that consisted of completing a checklist of things I had to do and see. This Style 1 was consistent with my task-relevant readiness, in that I was unable (lacking the knowledge, experience, and skills to be an underway OD) and unwilling (in the sense that I was apprehensive). The checklist did two things. It addressed my lack of knowledge and skills by providing a structure for learning my new job; it also addressed my apprehension, in that I could see that there was a systematic way to qualify as an OD.

For example, on the checklist was the task of visiting the ship's magazines where the ammunition for the five-inch gun mount was stored. I was met by a gunnersmate who took me on the tour and made sure I understood how the alarm system worked. He, like most of the other people I met, used a Style 2 leadership style to give the information while also offering encouragement. This was appropriate for my task-relevant readiness, in that I was unable, lacking knowledge of the armory and the alarm systems, but willing to learn.

The Style 2 continued when we got under way. I was assigned to stand watches with the qualified ODs as they stood their watches. Once again, I was treated with Style 2 leadership by each of the qualified ODs, and I was given more and more responsibility as I learned my role. Eventually, the qualified ODs would let me run the watch as if I were actually in charge. This represented a shift to Style 3, where there was some ongoing direction but mostly support and reinforcement of what I was doing right.

Of course, there was some movement back to Style 2 whenever I was asked questions; if I answered properly, I received a positive comment as the leaders returned to a Style 3. For instance, the qualified OD asked me, "What would you do if you saw a light on the horizon?"

My response was, "If the lookout hadn't reported it yet, I would make sure he knew where to look. I would contact the Combat Information Center and ask if they had identified anything on the radar that would correspond to the light. I would then proceed to the bridge wing and get a bearing to the light. I would also check the surface search radar to see if I could see if anything appeared there." The OD would say something like, "Great job." If I had left something out, he would have reminded me of what I should have done.

I received more and more responsibility until I was ready to stand a four-hour watch on my own. I was given the 4:00 P.M. to 8:00 P.M. watch, since not much was going on then, and I had access to the other officers without having to wake them. The operations officer, who was also the navigator, visited me during this first watch, as did the executive officer. They were there to offer support, as I was able but somewhat apprehensive standing my first watch on my own. I greatly appreciated their psychological support as I stood my first watch as an underway Officer of the Deck.

When I stood my next watch, I was on my own, but I did notice that the most experienced quartermaster had been assigned to my bridge team as a backup system, should I need any direction or support. At that moment, I was willing and able to assume my role as a qualified OD.

Tips on Leadership

Here are some tips to help you apply the ideas behind the Situational Leadership Model:

- Situational Leadership is a powerful model for assessing readiness and choosing the appropriate leadership style.
- Leadership style is the amount of task behavior (direction) and relationship behavior (support) that a leader provides a follower.

- Readiness is the ability and willingness of the employee to do a specific task.
- Leadership begins with your identifying the key tasks that each of your employees needs to do to be successful.
- By observing each employee's work, you can assess their readiness levels to do each important task.
- One of the keys to developing your people is to have clearly defined performance expectations that you determine for low-readiness-level employees (R1 and R2) but negotiate with high-readiness-level employees (R3 and R4).
- People develop in a logical manner and regress in a logical manner as well. If you've been using a Style 4, begin your leadership intervention by backing up to Style 3 and asking open-ended questions. Move back one style at a time as necessary.

APPLICATION EXERCISE

For each of your employees, list the agreed-upon activities determined in the Chapter 1 exercise. Assess the readiness level of each employee to do each task. Then ask each employee to describe how willing and able he or she is to do each task, and compare the results. Figure 2-6 will give you the structure you need to complete this exercise. (For a larger version of this and the other application exercise forms, visit www.aboutiwp.com.)

FIGURE 2-6. ACTIVITIES AND READINESS EXERCISE

Name: ______________________________

List the five to seven most important tasks (activities) needed to be done to be successful on the job, and then indicate your willingness and ability to do each task. *Ability* is defined by your knowledge, experience, and skills necessary to do the task. *Willingness* is defined by your desire and confidence to do the task.

1. ______________________________ able/unable
   ______________________________ willing/unwilling
2. ______________________________ able/unable
   ______________________________ willing/unwilling
3. ______________________________ able/unable
   ______________________________ willing/unwilling
4. ______________________________ able/unable
   ______________________________ willing/unwilling
5. ______________________________ able/unable
   ______________________________ willing/unwilling
6. ______________________________ able/unable
   ______________________________ willing/unwilling
7. ______________________________ able/unable
   ______________________________ willing/unwilling

Notes

1. Paul Hersey, Kenneth H. Blanchard, and Dewey E. Johnson, *Management of Organizational Behavior*, 8th ed. (Upper Saddle River, N.J.: Prentice-Hall, 2000).
2. Paul Hersey and Roger Chevalier, "Situational Leadership and Performance Coaching," in *Coaching for Leadership*, eds. Marshall Goldsmith, Laurence Lyons, and Alyssa Freas (San Francisco: Jossey-Bass Pfeiffer, 2000).

> "Advice is like snow; the softer it falls, the longer it dwells upon, and deeper it sinks into the mind."
>
> —SAMUEL TAYLOR COLERIDGE

CHAPTER 3

The Manager as Counselor

One of a manager's most important roles is that of counseling employees during, and especially at the end of, the performance-appraisal period. This chapter presents the Performance Counseling Guide, an aid to guide managers in formal interviewing, counseling, and coaching situations that is particularly relevant for end-of-period counseling sessions. Based on the Situational Leadership Model, the guide is divided into two phases, one that focuses on assessing an employee's readiness and the other that involves choosing an appropriate leadership style.

The Performance Counseling Guide

The Performance Counseling Guide is one of several guides developed by the author that apply Situational Leadership for specific purposes such as coaching, selling, and customer service. The full guide is shown in Figure 3-4, but for purposes of instruction here, we'll construct the guide in a series of steps.

Phase 1: Assessment of Follower Readiness

The Performance Counseling Guide uses leadership Styles 4, 3, and 2 (S4, S3, and S2) to prepare for the counseling session, to open lines of communication, and to diagnose employee readiness for the tasks involved. Figure 3-1 shows the three steps of this phase that will be developed step-by-step.

During the performance-appraisal period, employees may perceive a lot of Style 4 behavior, as you have limited interaction with them as you observe, monitor, and track their performance. You may intervene occasionally to give direction when necessary and to recognize positive performance, but the overall atmosphere is that of low direction and low support for most of the period. That experience continues as you prepare for the counseling session that ends the period. At this point, you review relevant materials, such as your performance records.

1. Observe, monitor, and track performance.
2. Review your records and employee input.
3. Set counseling goals; develop a strategy.

In most cases, you should next move to Style 3 to begin the assessment, increasing your support for the employee by building rapport, opening up lines of communication, and reinforcing the employee's positive performance or potential. One important objective of this step is to identify how the employee perceives any shortfalls in performance during the period. (If the employee sees the shortfall the same way as you do, you will use Style 2 to work with the individual to improve future performance. If the employee does not recognize the problem, you will most likely need to intervene with Style 1, using your documentation to show a pattern of unacceptable behavior and its impact on the performance of your workgroup.)

1. Build rapport, trust, and personal power.
2. Begin session with open-ended questions.
3. Identify issues and problem ownership.

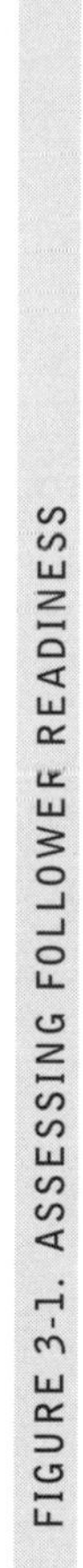

FIGURE 3-1. ASSESSING FOLLOWER READINESS

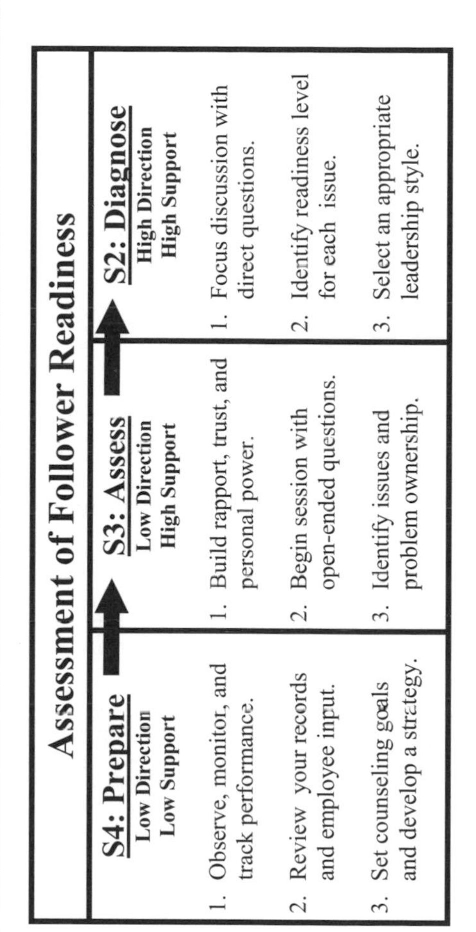

You then move to Style 2 for the diagnosis, to focus the discussion with direct questions that will help you to gain further insight into the employee's perception of performance and to identify the employee's view of any shortcomings. For each task critical for the employee's success, you must assess the employee's readiness (ability and willingness) level so you can choose the best leadership style for intervention.

1. Focus discussion with direct questions.
2. Identify readiness level for each issue.
3. Select an appropriate leadership style.

Phase 2: Choice of Leadership Style

After assessing each employee's readiness for the critical tasks, you can select the appropriate leadership style to achieve the desired result. Figure 3-2 presents the range of employee readiness.

As with the Situational Leadership Model, the critical tasks must be clearly defined before a readiness level can be determined. As shown in Figure 3-3, if the employee is unable and unwilling or insecure (R1) or does not recognize his or her own poor performance, you will need to use Style 1 to communicate the performance shortfall and its impact on the rest of the workgroup (Prescribe). The employee's role should be defined in terms of the means (the activities that are necessary to be successful) and the ends (the goals that should be achieved). You will need to inform, describe, instruct, and direct the employee as you communicate expectations for performance.

FIGURE 3-2. RANGE OF EMPLOYEE READINESS

Able & willing & confident	Able but unwilling or insecure	Unable but willing or confident	Unable & unwilling or insecure
R4	**R3**	**R2**	**R1**

FIGURE 3-3. SELECTING A LEADERSHIP STYLE

S4: Follow Up Low Direction Low Support	S3: Reinforce Low Direction High Support	S2: Develop High Direction High Support	S1: Prescribe High Direction Low Support
1. Document session in performance record. 2. Follow through on all commitments. 3. Observe, monitor, and track performance.	1. Reinforce self-worth and self-esteem. 2. Assess understanding and commitment. 3. Encourage, support, motivate, and empower.	1. Discuss activities/goals to improve performance. 2. Reach agreement on best course of action. 3. Guide, persuade, explain, and train.	1. Clearly communicate expectations and goals. 2. Define role as both means and ends. 3. Inform, describe, instruct, and direct.
Selection of Leader's Style Matched to Follower Readiness			
Able & willing & confident	Able but unwilling or insecure	Unable but willing or confident	Unable & unwilling or insecure
R4	**R3**	**R2**	**R1**

1. Clearly communicate expectations and goals.
2. Define role as both means and ends.
3. Inform, describe, instruct, and direct.

If the employee is unable but is willing or confident (R2), or sees the performance shortfall the way that you do, use Style 2 to develop the employee as you discuss ways to improve (Develop). You will need to reach agreement as to the best course of action in terms of what the employee needs to do and what you will do. The Style 2 choice is characterized by terms such as *guide, persuade, explain*, and *train*, all of which help develop the employee.

1. Discuss goals to improve performance.
2. Reach agreement on best course of action.
3. Guide, persuade, explain, and train.

If the employee is able but unwilling or insecure, Style 3 should be used to give the needed support and encouragement (Reinforce). The employee needs high amounts of support but only low amounts of direction. The Style 3 choice will reinforce the employee's feelings of confidence, self-worth, and self-esteem. Style 3 leadership is characterized by terms such as *encourage, support, motivate,* and *empower.*

1. Reinforce self-worth and self-esteem.
2. Assess understanding and commitment.
3. Encourage, support, motivate, and empower.

The final step in the counseling process is to follow up on commitments that you made and the written appraisal, if this was an end-of-period counseling session. Style 4 is used to follow up on the meeting as you return to observing, monitoring, and tracking performance (Follow Up).

1. Document session in performance record.
2. Follow through on all commitments.
3. Observe, monitor, and track performance.

The combined assessment and selection model is shown in Figure 3-3 and summarizes the steps of the process.

Putting the Performance Counseling Guide to Use

The Performance Counseling Guide, as shown in Figure 3-4, is the complete performance aid that merges follower readiness and leadership style. While the intervention style is chosen based on the employee's readiness, the manager's goal is to develop the employee by using successive leadership styles as the manager moves from steps of prescribing, to developing, to reinforcing, and then to following up.

All too often, managers neglect to take the time to assess employee readiness, and the employee becomes defensive, with little subsequent hope for improved performance. The assessment phase is critical to the coaching process, in that the manager must prepare, assess, and diagnose prior to intervening. In effect, the manager must "earn the right" to intervene.

In addition to assessing the employee's readiness level for each task, it's important to determine "who owns the problem." If you see a performance shortfall but the employee doesn't, the Style 1 intervention is appropriate: You describe the problem and its implications to the employee. If you both own the problem—that is, if you both see the problem for what it is—the Style 2 intervention is called for as you work together to resolve the problem. If the employee sees a problem, such as conflicting performance expectations from the workgroup, but it has not affected the employee's performance, the Style 3 intervention is appropriate as you support the employee in resisting the expectations of the group. If neither of you sees a problem, then the Style 4 action is in order, since there is nothing to correct or support.

A key to making your assessments work is the way in which you ask questions.[1]

FIGURE 3-4. THE PERFORMANCE COUNSELING GUIDE SHOWING LEADERSHIP STYLE MATCHED TO FOLLOWER READINESS

Performance Counseling Guide

Assessment of Follower Readiness

S4: Prepare Low Direction Low Support	S3: Assess Low Direction High Support	S2: Diagnose High Direction High Support
1. Observe, monitor, and track performance.	1. Build rapport, trust, and personal power.	1. Focus discussion with direct questions.
2. Review your records and employee input.	2. Begin session with open-ended questions.	2. Identify readiness level for each issue.
3. Set counseling goals and develop a strategy.	3. Identify issues and problem ownership.	3. Select an appropriate leadership style.

S4: Follow Up Low Direction Low Support	S3: Reinforce Low Direction High Support	S2: Develop High Direction High Support	S1: Prescribe High Direction Low Support
1. Document session in performance record.	1. Reinforce self-worth and self-esteem.	1. Discuss activities/goals to improve performance.	1. Clearly communicate expectations and goals.
2. Follow through on all commitments.	2. Assess understanding and commitment.	2. Reach agreement on best course of action.	2. Define role as both means and ends.
3. Observe, monitor, and track performance.	3. Encourage, support, motivate, and empower.	3. Guide, persuade, explain, and train.	3. Inform, describe, instruct, and direct.

Selection of Leader's Style Matched to Follower Readiness

Able & willing & confident	Able but unwilling or insecure	Unable but willing or confident	Unable & unwilling or insecure
R4	**R3**	**R2**	**R1**

As shown in Figure 3-5, you start with open-ended questions to assess the overall situation, using Style 3 as your guide. Then you follow up with direct questions to assess the performance shortfall and its causes.

Perhaps the best way to show how to work with others to assess performance is to give another example from my years in the U.S. Coast Guard. I was sitting in my office when my senior instructor came in. We were in the first week of a leadership and management course for junior officers. We had presented similar material to senior enlisted personnel in three programs, but this was our first junior officer class.

My senior instructor sat down in the chair in front of my desk and said, "We have a problem."

"What's that?" I asked.

He said, "Bob Smith doesn't want to teach the Critical Path Method tomorrow."

"He's taught it three times before. What's his problem?" I asked.

"I'm not sure, but I think he's worried about teaching the junior officers," he responded. "He's afraid that with most of them having engineering backgrounds, they'll know more about the subject than he does."

"What do you think we should do?" I asked.

"Maybe you can talk with him. I've tried, but haven't gotten anywhere," he responded.

"Let him know that I'd like to see him," I told my senior instructor.

I took some time to think about the chief's readiness level. He was definitely R4 for teaching the enlisted courses and knew the material cold. What had changed was the audience. I should have seen this coming, but I hadn't spent enough time working with him to prepare him.

He showed up outside my door and said, "You wanted to see me?"

I said, "Come on in." He sat down, and I sat in the other chair in front of my desk with him. "I understand that you have some reservations about teaching CPM tomorrow."

"I don't have reservations. I just won't do it," he said.

My natural inclination was to shift to a Style 1 and tell him he had to do it, but

FIGURE 3-5. QUESTIONING TECHNIQUES AND ASSESSMENT OF FOLLOWER READINESS

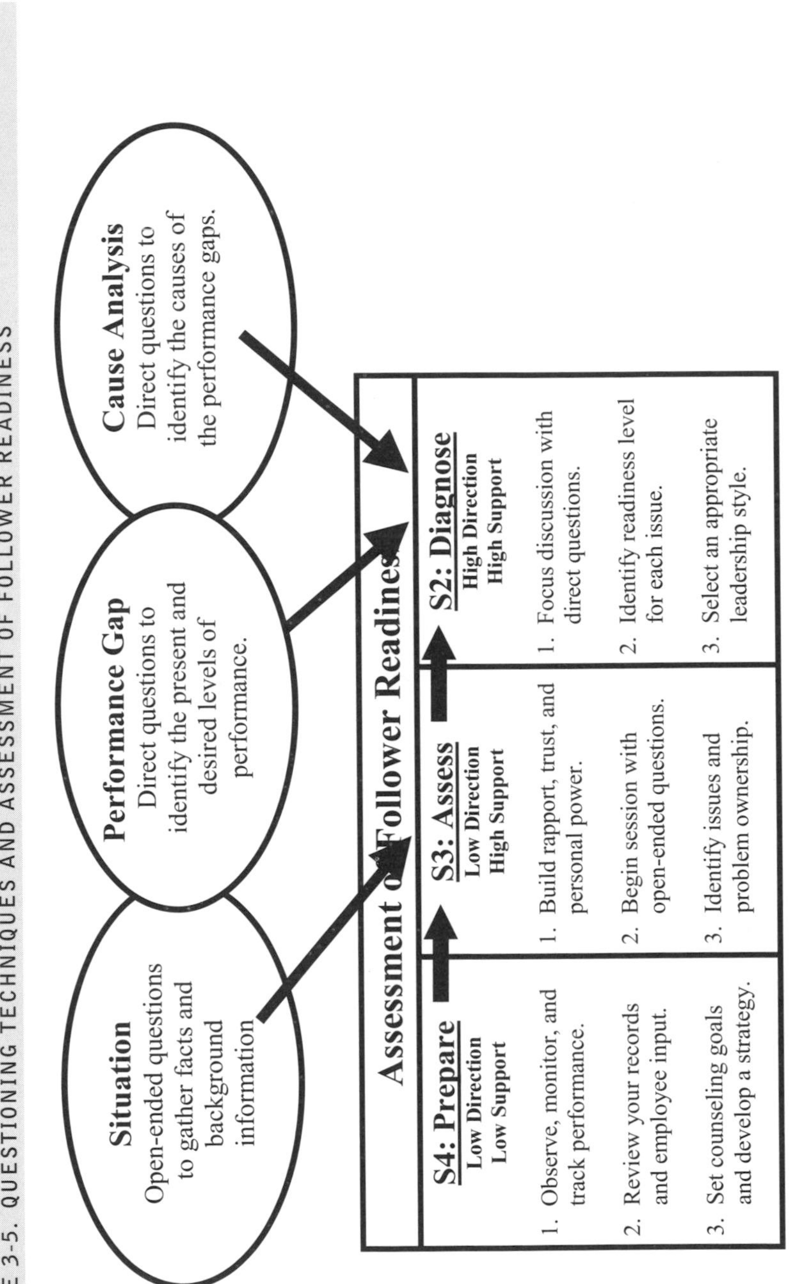

I knew that I needed more than compliance if this was going to work. So I decided to stay with Style 3 and ask more questions to get a better handle on the situation.

"Why don't you want to teach?" I asked. "You've done a great job of presenting CPM in the last three classes."

"Those were enlisted men, and they didn't have any background in the material. These guys are all engineers and probably have had college courses in it."

He had confirmed the problem. We talked for about 15 minutes, with my explaining that all of the officers had been out of college for at least three years and had forgotten more than they remembered about the subject. I kept on giving positive feedback on his past performance as I reminded him that no one else was qualified to teach the subject.

Finally, when I thought I got through to him, I said, "It's going to be either you or me who will teach CPM tomorrow, and you're better qualified than I am. I can live with your decision. Who is it going to be?"

He said, "I'll do it, but you will have to be my backup instructor."

He was still R3 even though he was willing to take on the role; he was able, but he lacked the confidence that he had when teaching the enlisted personnel. So, I had to be in the class with him in case something went wrong. As it turned out, he did his usual great performance, getting lots of great comments from the class. He just needed some support to get him through. If I had been really paying attention, I probably could have avoided the situation by anticipating the problem. Fortunately, I was able to adjust my leadership style to the situation and work with him to get the results we both wanted.

Tips on Counseling

Use the following tips to help put the ideas presented in this chapter into practice.

- Recognize that assessment is the key to counseling; this includes preparing for the meeting properly, building rapport with your employees, asking open-ended questions, and then asking direct questions.

- Prepare for the counseling session by reviewing your notes, talking with peers and seniors about the employee's performance, reviewing the employee's input, setting goals for the meeting, preparing some open-ended questions, and picking an appropriate time and place for the counseling session.
- Assess the overall situation as you begin the counseling session by building rapport, asking open-ended questions to learn how the employee perceived his or her performance, and identifying where you are in agreement or disagreement regarding the employee's performance.
- Diagnose by "drilling down" with direct questions to determine performance gaps and causes while you identify whether the employee recognizes performance shortfalls and determine the employee's readiness for the specific tasks needed to be successful on the job.
- Prescribe solutions when the employee does not recognize the performance shortfall and when you see a problem and the employee doesn't; confront with facts about the employee's performance and give ways to improve.
- Develop the employee after the employee becomes aware of the performance shortfall and is ready to improve; discuss and reach agreement on the desired activities and results as well as the best way to proceed.
- Reinforce the employee's feelings of self-worth and self-esteem while recognizing the employee's positive performance and willingness to improve.
- Follow up on all commitments you have made, document the counseling session, and write the appraisal if this was an end-of-period counseling session.
- Adjust your leadership style (the amount of direction and support you give) to the match the employee's readiness level (willingness and ability) for each important task.
- Maintain a positive work environment where your employees believe they have an opportunity to succeed every day.

APPLICATION EXERCISE

To use what you have learned in this chapter, you will need to hold a counseling session with at least one of your employees. The most logical people to consider are employees who are due for their annual performance review and employees whose performance you'd like to improve.

Prepare: Start your preparation by reviewing any records you have regarding the individual's performance. These records can include notes you have made throughout the period, memos or letters received from other divisions or customers regarding the individual's performance, and internal reports with measures of the employee's performance reflecting productivity and quality of work.

Reflect on the employee's performance and develop open-ended questions to begin a discussion of it. Examples might be, "How have things been going for you on the shop floor?" Or, "Have you had any problems in doing your job lately?"

Assess: Think about the purpose of the counseling session and determine how much rapport you should build with the employee. If the counseling session is to correct a number of performance shortfalls, limit the time you spend building rapport. If the counseling session is to provide feedback to a good performer, spend more time in building rapport.

Once you have opened up communications by building rapport with the employee, find out how the employee feels about the performance. This is when you use your open-ended questions. As the employee answers, listen closely and identify areas for where you can ask more direct questions. Try to identify whether the employee sees the same areas for improvement as you do.

Diagnose: Listen closely to determine whether the employee sees his or her performance the same way as you do. Determine the employee's readiness level to change. If the employee does not see the performance issue that you see, define your expectations and give details of how the employee has performed (S1: Prescribe). If you both see the problem, discuss ways to improve (S2: Develop). If you both agree that performance has been acceptable, reinforce that performance by praising the employee (S3: Reinforce).

Prescribe: Only use Style 1 when necessary, such as when the employee doesn't see the problem or is unwilling and unable to change. You may need to confront the employee using your records to show the pattern of poor performance and the impact that poor performance is having on your workgroup. An example would be, "During the past month you have been late four times. Although you have had an excuse for each time, this pattern of performance is not acceptable. Not only are you not here on time, but by being late, other members of your workgroup cannot do their jobs. The workday starts at 8:00 A.M. That means you are here and ready to work by 8:00 A.M."

You may also use this intervention to assign a new role to an employee. Tell the employee what the new job entails in terms of what is to be done, how it should be done, where it should be done, and who else is involved.

Develop: If you are working with a motivated employee, you may be able to bypass the Prescribe step and move directly to the Develop stage. This is true if you and the employee both recognize a performance issue. Rather than tell a good employee what needs to be done, you can discuss the issue and ask for input as to what should be done to improve performance. This allows the employee to participate in deciding what should be done.

Reinforce: With experienced employees who are highly motivated, the counseling session is to reinforce performance. For those tasks where there is no need for improvement, you can move directly to reinforcement. For those individuals you have worked to develop, use this stage to convey your confidence that performance will improve.

Follow Up: You must do whatever you committed to do during the interview. You should also record a summary of the interview that includes when and where the counseling took place, the issues discussed, and the planned course of action.

Note

1. Paul Hersey and Roger Chevalier, "Situational Leadership and Executive Coaching," *Coaching for Leadership,* 2nd ed., eds. Marshall Goldsmith and Laurence Lyons (San Francisco: Pfeiffer, 2006).

"Coaches who can outline plays on a black board are a dime a dozen. The ones who win get inside their players and motivate."

—VINCE LOMBARDI

CHAPTER 4

Motivating Your Players

One of the most challenging roles you have as a manager is that of keeping your people motivated. But how do you get inside their heads to keep them motivated? An underlying principle for improving workplace performance is that motivation comes from within the individual, not from outside. Yet as a manager, you are an outsider. So, to motivate your employees, you must identify their underlying needs and create a work environment in which these needs can be fulfilled. The challenge is that each person has different needs and, therefore, different motivators. As was the case with leadership style, you have to adjust your means of creating a motivating work environment to meet the unique needs of your people.

This chapter presents an analysis of human needs, particularly as applied to the workplace, and then gives you tips on how to apply that knowledge to motivate your employees by identifying and meeting their needs in the work environment where possible.

Individual Needs and Motivation

The relationship between an employee's needs and how he or she is motivated is depicted in Figure 4-1. The employee would like to satisfy a certain underlying

FIGURE 4-1. SATISFACTION OF INDIVIDUAL NEEDS

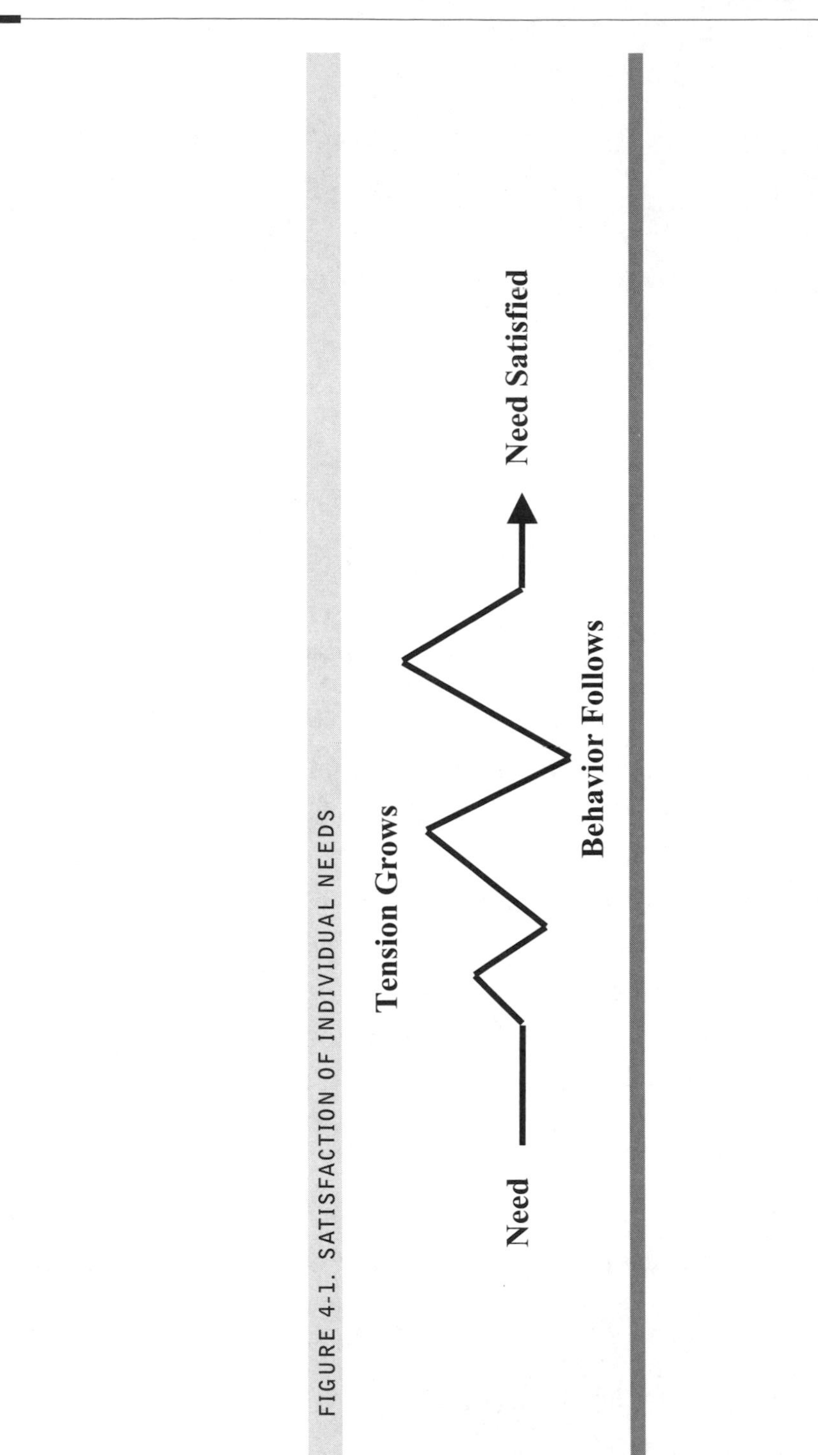

need. If this need is not immediately satisfied, tension grows and then behavior follows as the employee tries to relieve the tension and satisfy the need. In the simplest situations, the need is satisfied quickly.

For example, suppose an employee has a need for a cup of coffee because of thirst, habit, and/or caffeine addiction. Tension grows when the employee realizes that no one has brewed a pot of coffee that morning. The employee could wait for someone else to brew the coffee, but decides to make the coffee. Tension grows as, drop by drop, the coffee falls into the pot. The employee then switches the pot with a coffee cup to fill the cup before the pot fills. The need is finally satisfied.

Another example of how needs cause behavior is how individuals form long-term relationships, such as marriage. Many different needs are met when two people enter a long-term relationship. Companionship is certainly one of these needs, but, for many people, so is security. In some cases, one spouse enters into the relationship to fulfill different needs from those of the other spouse. The relationship continues as long as each spouse's needs are taken care of to a reasonable degree.

This process of needs fulfillment is straightforward until a barrier arises between the individual and satisfaction of an underlying need. The barrier builds tension to the point where the employee may find a substitute for the original need. Figure 4-2 illustrates how individuals find alternative ways to satisfy their needs through substitution.

For example, suppose a husband and wife have different social needs. If the wife has stronger social needs than were being met by her husband, she might spend more time with her friends or join a club or church group. These are socially acceptable means around a barrier to satisfying a need, and they are referred to as *substitution.* But some people may do things that are not socially acceptable to satisfy frustrated needs or to relieve tension. In the case of our married couple, this might take the form of an affair. The term to describe this type of action is *maladaptive behavior*, which is a form of socially unacceptable substitution. In the case of our married couple, maladaptive behavior can take the form of having an affair or can be directed toward relieving the tension (drug or alcohol abuse). Figure 4-3 extends the earlier figure to include maladaptive behavior.

(text continued on page 58)

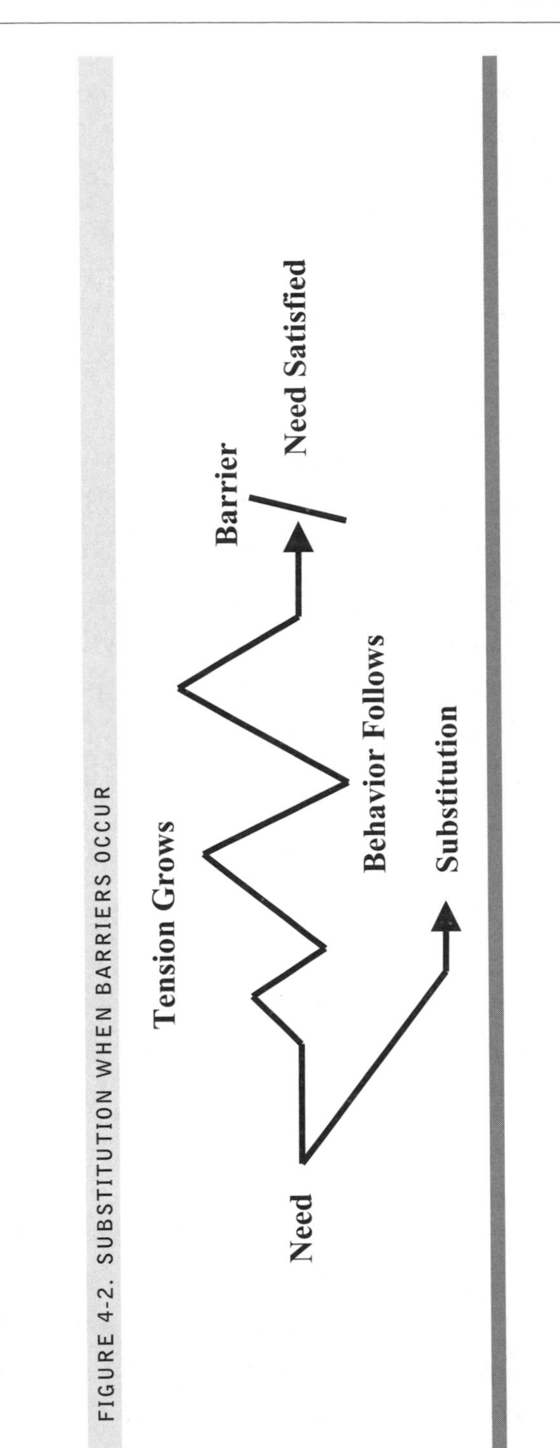

FIGURE 4-2. SUBSTITUTION WHEN BARRIERS OCCUR

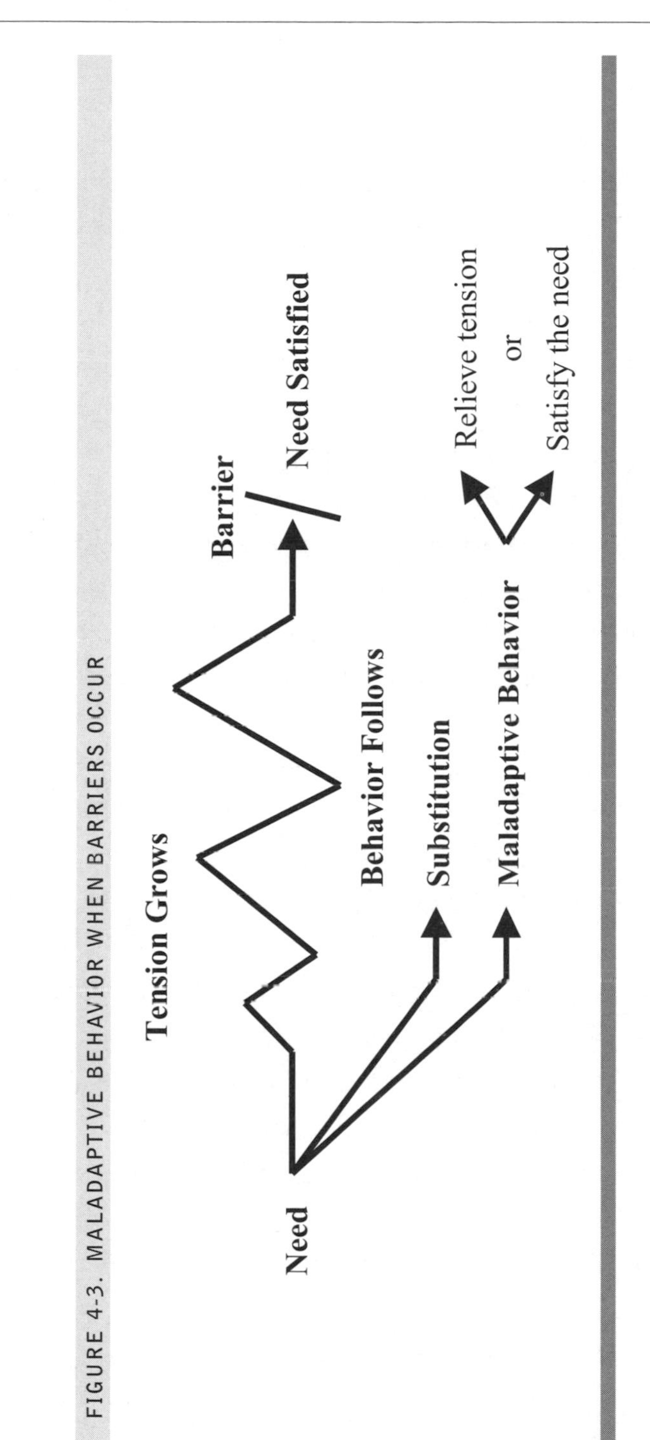

FIGURE 4-3. MALADAPTIVE BEHAVIOR WHEN BARRIERS OCCUR

If substitution and/or maladaptive behavior do not satisfy the need, or at least relieve the tension, *abandonment* may result. This is the case when all hope of satisfying a need in the present situation has been exhausted. For the married couple, this could manifest itself as divorce or remaining in a loveless marriage. Figure 4-4 depicts abandonment.

The classic example of abandonment comes from the behavioral sciences, with an experiment that focused on a pike, a carnivorous fish. Researchers initially fed the pike live minnows, which the pike would chase and eventually eat. They then placed a piece of plate glass in the tank and put the minnows on the other side. The pike could see its dinner but could not get to it. The pike beat its head on the glass divider repeatedly, but eventually it gave up and settled down to the bottom of the tank. The experimenters didn't want the pike to die, so they took the plate glass out and the minnows eventually swam around the entire tank. The pike literally starved in the midst of plenty, having abandoned all hope of satisfying its needs in that environment.

But what does this look like on the job? Ideally, employees have their needs satisfied on the job to a reasonable degree. But if an employee has a need, such as that for recognition, and it is not satisfied on the job, that employee may seek roles outside the workplace to fulfill that need. Substitution may take the form of directing energy both on and off the job to roles that provide recognition. For example, an employee may spend time on the job doing volunteer work that receives more recognition than work on the job.

Maladaptive behavior can take the form of lateness or absenteeism, but it can also be a factor in alcohol or drug abuse. Abandonment can be seen when employees quit to find other work that may better meet their needs. Or they may "retire on the job," working but not motivated to do a better job since they have abandoned hope of satisfying their needs in that environment.

Maslow's Hierarchy of Needs

Fortunately, a person's needs do not appear in random fashion but rather in a hierarchy or ranking of importance. The behavioral psychologist Abraham Maslow de-

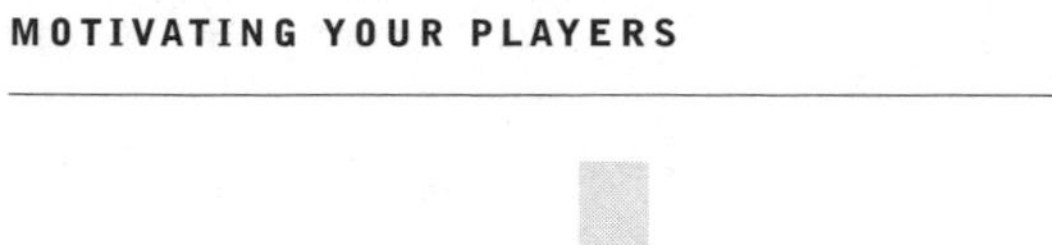

FIGURE 4-4. ABANDONMENT WHEN BARRIERS OCCUR

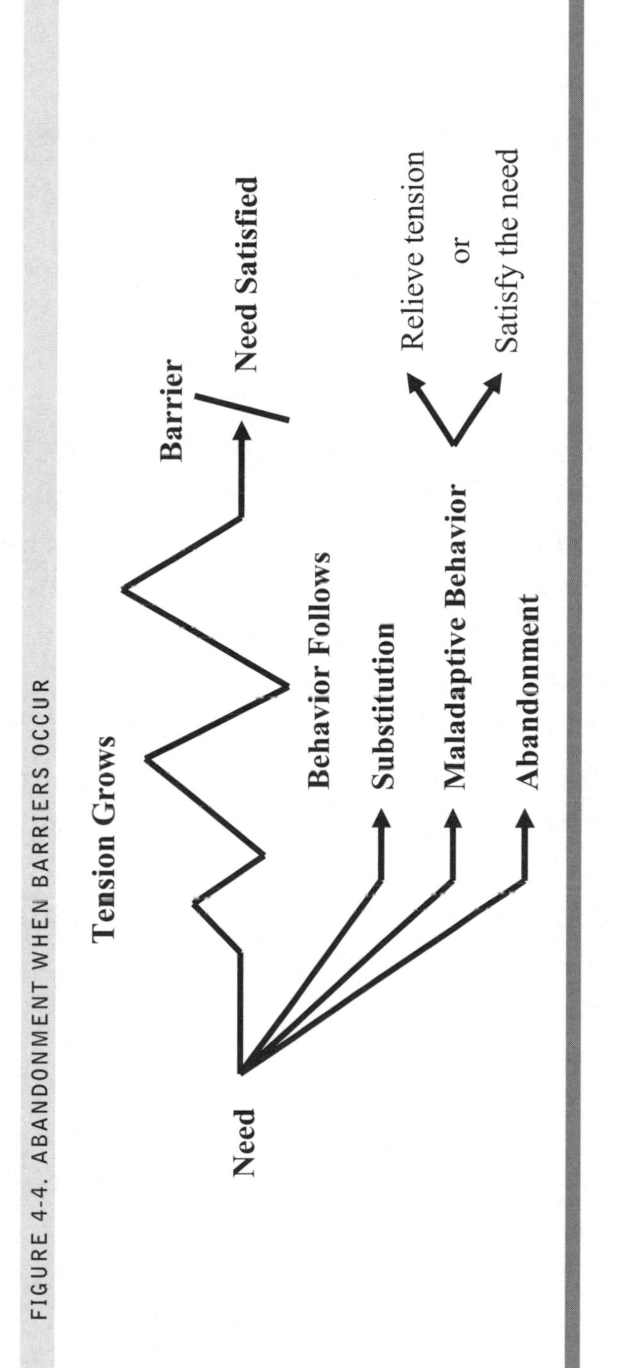

scribed seven different levels of need that cause individuals to prioritize their needs and thus to have different motivations in different circumstances.[1] Most management books discuss only the five detailed below, omitting the remaining two because they do not readily apply to the workplace. Those final two are the need for *spirituality* and the need for the *aesthetic* (balance, order, and beauty). Figure 4-5 shows the hierarchy of needs.

Here are the needs that apply more to the work environment:

- *Survival/Physiological*: This is the most basic level of need, for air, water, food, shelter, and sex. These needs result from our physical makeup. Severe financial or health problems can drive a worker to operate at this needs level.
- *Security*: This needs level extends survival need into the future. While survival is centered on the here and now, security is based on having survival needs fulfilled in the longer term.
- *Social*: This need level is centered on relationships with other people. Each of us is different as to how much social contact we need; the stronger your social needs, the more you will bend to the will of the group to gain acceptance.
- *Esteem*: This needs level can be divided into esteem of others and self-esteem. You must balance these esteems in your life so that you do not ignore the comments of others but at the same time are not immobilized by what others say.
- *Self-actualization*: This needs level is the desire to become all that we can become. It is characterized on the job by enjoying the work itself while experiencing autonomy and professional growth.

Even though Maslow's two other needs have been left out of most management books, there is a growing realization that those needs, too, can be important (and satisfied) in the workplace. But the classic five-layer hierarchy is unquestionably helpful in understanding employee behavior on the job. Employees do their best work when they are working at jobs that satisfy their higher-level needs, which means they are in jobs that they enjoy and are challenged to do their best. But the lower needs levels can be distracting if not met. For example, an employee who

FIGURE 4-5. MASLOW'S HIERARCHY OF NEEDS

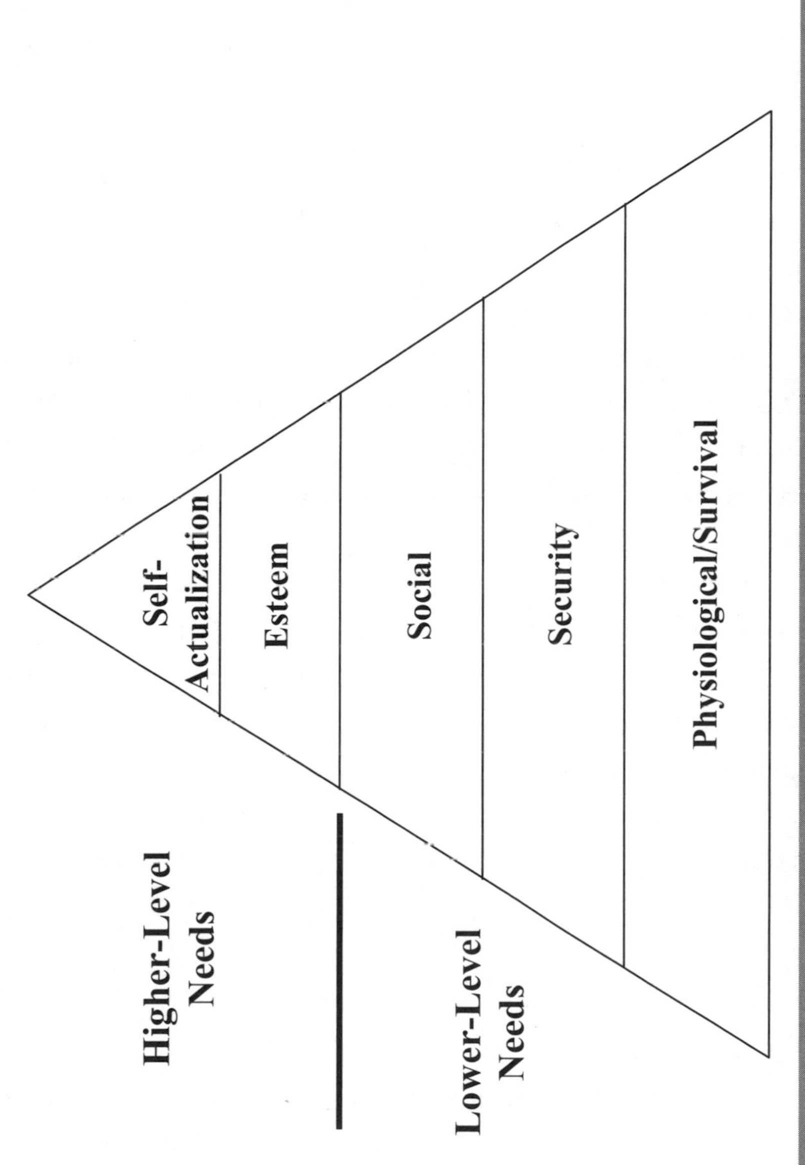

has health problems will no longer work effectively. Similarly, if an employee is experiencing a dramatic change in his or her personal life, security and social needs take over as the most important, and the quality of work will usually decline.

Putting the Needs Hierarchy to Work

In addition to helping managers understand why employees do what they do, the hierarchy of needs can help you determine appropriate forms of recognition. People operating at lower needs levels should be given tangible rewards such as money and gift certificates. If social needs are the most important, then group recognition is in order. Those on the esteem-needs level respond best to plaques and honors, while those who are at the self-actualizing level are not as interested in traditional rewards, since they get greater satisfaction from the work itself. It is also critical to remember how quickly circumstances can change needs levels, so recognition that is appropriate at one moment may become inappropriate at another.

As you think about your employees, also think about yourself. Are your lower-level needs for survival, security, and social interaction being met in your work? Do you have the opportunity to get positive recognition and to grow on the job? Are your higher-level needs being met in your work environment? For your employees, you are a major component of their work environment. Have you and the organization created a work environment where your people can satisfy their needs on the job?

Satisfaction on the Job

In an attempt to determine what factors lead to worker job satisfaction, psychologist Frederick Herzberg conducted a study in which people were asked to describe their most satisfying and dissatisfying experiences on the job and to give the reasons why.[2] They also were asked to describe their levels of performance in the two experiences.

Think about a time when you were most satisfied on the job. It could be your present job, or a past job in the same or a different organization. What made the job so satisfying? What was the quality of your work? Similarly, think about a time when you were most dissatisfied on the job. What made the job dissatisfying? What was the quality of your work? Was it as good as when you worked at the job where more of your needs were met?

When these questions were asked of large groups of people, two different sets of factors typically appeared where responses were analyzed. We call these sets of work issues *motivators* and *maintenance factors.* For motivators, certain factors related to the satisfaction of higher-level needs (esteem and self-actualization) appear frequently when individuals describe their most satisfying experiences on the job:

- *Achievement*: Employees indicated that they were accomplishing something of genuine value on the job.
- *Recognition*: Employees indicated that they received appropriate recognition for their work.
- *Responsibility*: Employees indicated that they had responsibility for their work or the work of others.
- *Work itself*: Employees indicated that the work itself was enjoyable.
- *Advancement*: Employees indicated that the job led to a promotion or a better position.
- *Personal growth*: Employees indicated that they learned new knowledge or skills as a result of having the job.

While each factor was not present in every description of an individual's most satisfying experience, nearly all included at least one of the factors. These factors became known as *motivators* since the surveyed individuals indicated that they were performing their jobs at a very high level. The impact of motivators is felt on the job for a long time. How many of these factors were present when you had your most satisfying work experience?

Dissatisfaction on the Job

In the same survey, these same people described their least satisfying experience on the job. The factors that appeared were not the absence of motivators but the presence of a different group of factors. These latter factors were originally called *hygiene factors*, reflecting Herzberg's earliest work with the pharmaceutical industry. He used the analogy of hygiene as being a way to avoid illness (dissatisfaction on the job) and because the factors appear to be related to lower-level needs. These factors associated with dissatisfaction are now usually described as *maintenance factors* since they "maintain" people on the job but do not promote performance above minimal levels:

- *Policies and administration*: Employees indicated that they had problems with their organization's policies and administrative procedures.
- *Quality of supervision*: Employees indicated dissatisfaction with the quality of supervision they received.
- *Relationships with others*: Employees indicated dissatisfaction with the interpersonal relationships they had with seniors, peers, and subordinates.
- *Work conditions*: Employees indicated that they had problems with the work environment and conditions.
- *Salary*: Employees indicated that their salaries did not reflect their performance or their contributions to the organization.
- *Impact of the job on personal life*: Employees indicated that the job had an adverse effect on their personal lives.

How many of these factors were present when you had your least satisfying work experience?

What You Can Do

As a manager, you need to realize that you can maintain your employees by providing a safe and secure work environment where their lower-level needs are satisfied (maintenance factors). You can also motivate them when they have an opportunity to achieve, grow, and be recognized to satisfy higher-level needs. Maintenance factors will not motivate workers after the related lower-level needs are satisfied; motivators are necessary to sustain performance. Let's take a look at several types of motivators.

Job Enrichment

A technique that adds opportunities for employees to fulfill their higher-level needs is job enrichment. By enriching their jobs you can ensure more opportunities for them to take pride in what they are doing. Remember, of course, that you must ensure that their lower-level needs are met to some reasonable degree before attempting to enhance their jobs.

There are certain core dimensions of a job that come into play as you enrich the jobs that people are doing:[3]

- *Task identity*: Employees can identify more with the final product; they produce an identifiable product that they can take pride in making.
- *Task significance*: Employees can see how their work affects the finished product, the others whom they work with, and the customers who will use the product.
- *Variety of skills*: Employees use many different skills to complete their work.
- *Autonomy*: Employees make decisions regarding how the work process is done, such as the production schedule and procedures to do the job.
- *Feedback*: Employees receive timely, specific feedback on the quality of their work.
- *Responsibility*: Employees are given responsibility for the completion of the tasks.

Job enrichment has to be tailored to the situation. I once toured a plant where one group of workers was responsible for building test equipment that was used to calibrate other test equipment. The company was experiencing a high return rate for the test equipment that wasn't up to standard, and a high turnover of employees. Management was using an assembly-line means of production, in which each worker performed several simple tasks and passed the unit on to the next employee.

The manager went to his twenty employees and asked how the company could improve the quality of the work environment as well as the quality of the product. The suggestion was made that they end the assembly line and that each of the employees produce the final product individually. This change would require cross training all of the employees and more production equipment, but the change was made, with great success. Here's how the core dimensions of the job were changed:

1. Each employee could identify with the finished product since he or she now built the whole unit (task identity).
2. Each employee could see the significance of each of the steps since the individuals now built the whole unit themselves (task significance).
3. Each employee was required to use a wide variety of skills as he or she built the whole unit individually (variety of skills).
4. Employees were no longer dependent on each other. The shop went to flex-time, whereby employees could start and end each day when they wanted as long as they were there from 10:00 A.M. to 2:00 P.M. for training and lunch together. Employees who wanted to come in later or leave earlier than the old hours didn't have to ask permission as long as they worked eight hours each day (autonomy).
5. Each unit was inspected by Quality Assurance, and feedback was provided to the employee who built it. Additionally, the employee's initials were included in the unit's label and returned to the employee who built it if there was a return under the warranty (feedback).
6. Each employee took responsibility for the hours he or she kept and the quality of work done (responsibility).

Job Rotation and Job Enlargement

Job rotation is another way of adding motivators, addressing some of the core dimensions of a job. By moving your people through the various tasks that need to be done, they will gain a better understanding of the work (task identity) and will see its importance (task significance), and they will also expand their skills (variety of skills). Where job rotation falls short is in the areas of autonomy, feedback, and responsibility.

Job enlargement is when you add more work to an employee's job as a motivator. Remember, more is not always better. As you add more challenging work, you must also remove work. If you don't, the increased workload may upset the maintenance factors of work conditions and impact the employee's personal life. See Figure 4-6 for an illustration of effective job enlargement.

Recognition

The most powerful motivator you have is recognition. If used properly, recognition can shape the performance of employees and workgroups by recognizing exceptional performance that encourages others to improve their performance. For recognition to have successful results, the following points must be recognized:

- Recognition must be perceived by employees as being fair. If the same person is recognized all the time, and is the only person recognized, others will be less likely to improve. Sometimes it's better to reward "the most improved" rather than "the best."
- Recognition should be at the recipient's needs level. Trophies and plaques work well at the esteem-needs level, but more practical rewards are necessary for the security- or survival-needs levels.
- If employees have strong social needs, group recognition may be more appropriate than individual recognition.
- Recognition can be tangible or symbolic. A pen with the company logo works best as a reward if the only way you can get one is by receiving it as a reward. The military services have long used medals that cost about $20 to reward individuals for valor and exceptional performance.
- Some of the most motivating rewards cost the organization little or nothing. These include timely praise, more flexible hours and greater autonomy, greater

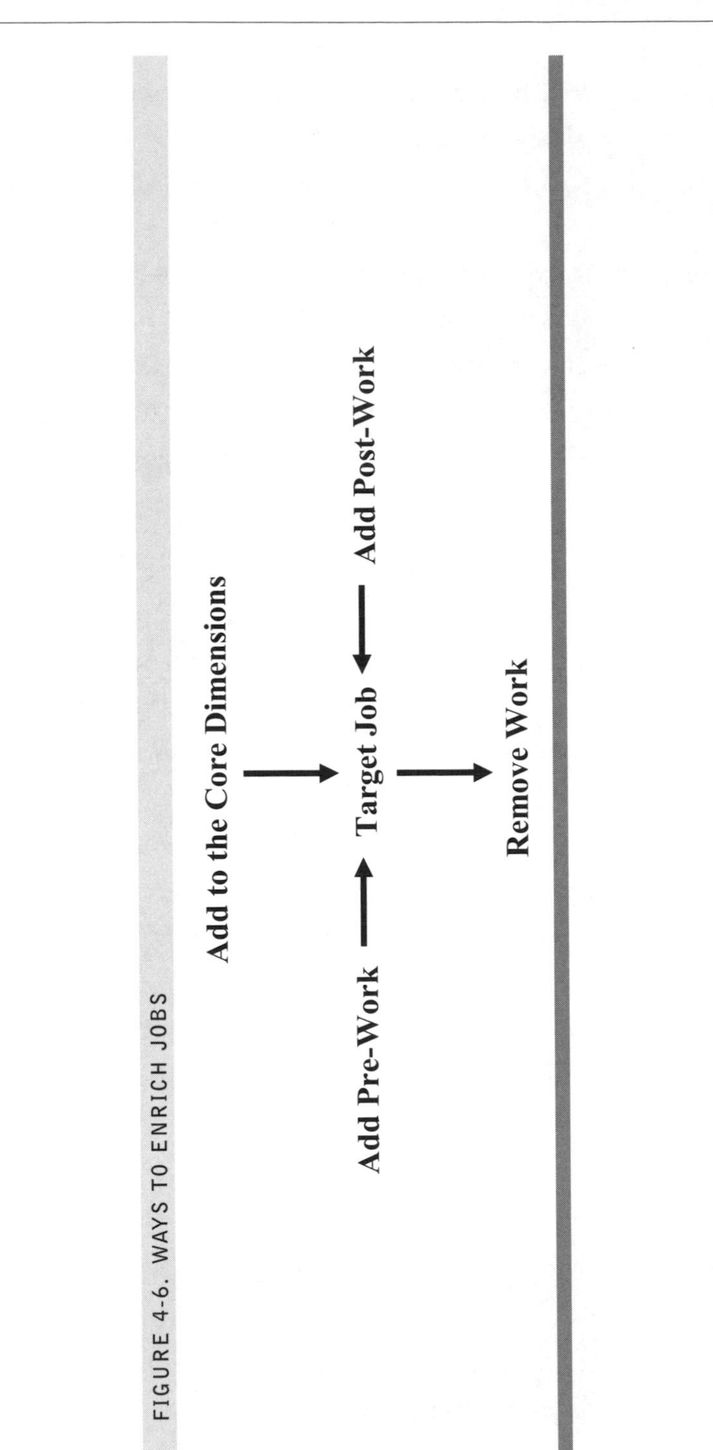

FIGURE 4-6. WAYS TO ENRICH JOBS

involvement in decision making, more challenging and interesting responsibilities, and training and development opportunities.

Recognition can be continuous or intermittent. *Continuous reinforcement* is when you give recognition every time the employee performs at a certain level. This can be useful as employees are learning their jobs and are at a low readiness level. Continuous reinforcement will shape the desired behavior quickly, but it may cause the employee to become dependent on recognition in order to continue good performance.

Intermittent reinforcement is when you provide recognition every second time, then every third time, then intermittently as the employee performs as required. The advantage is that while you are decreasing the external motivator (recognition), you are allowing employees to experience the internal motivators of a sense of achievement, greater responsibility for their work, enjoyment of the work itself, and personal growth.

The criteria for the recognition must be measurable and fixed so that employees know what is expected. By developing measurable criteria, management will clearly reinforce the standards of exceptional performance to all employees.

Tips on Motivation

The following tips will help you determine the best ways to motivate your employees.

- Motivation comes from within the employee; as a manager, you can create motion but not true motivation; individual needs and the tension of delayed satisfaction cause behavior.
- Each employee is different in terms of needs and what it will take in the workplace to satisfy these needs.
- If there's a barrier to satisfying a need on the job, employees may substitute, engage in maladaptive behavior, or engage in abandonment to cope with the lack of need satisfaction.

- Substitution is finding a socially acceptable way of meeting a need; maladaptive behavior is substitution that is not socially acceptable.
- Maladaptive behavior can be directed at the need or just at relieving the tension.
- Abandonment can lead to leaving a job or staying but giving up all hope of satisfying one's needs on the job: this is sometimes referred to as "being retired on the job."
- While Maslow described seven needs in his hierarchy, as managers you are primarily concerned with five: three lower-level needs of survival, safety, and social, and two higher-level needs of esteem and self-actualization.
- Maslow's lower-level needs correspond in the workplace to Herzberg's maintenance factors of policies and administration, quality of supervision, relationships with others, work conditions, salary, and impact of the job on personal life.
- Maslow's higher-level needs of esteem and self-actualization correspond to Herzberg's motivators of achievement, recognition, responsibility, enjoyment of the work itself, opportunity for advancement, and personal growth.
- The lower-level needs or maintenance factors must be satisfied before the employee can be moved to jobs that fulfill the higher-level needs and he or she can respond to the motivators.
- Job enrichment is a way of adding motivators to a job by giving the employee a greater sense of identifying with the finished product, understanding how tasks are related to the finished product, using a variety of skills, having autonomy, receiving timely feedback, and having personal responsibility for the work performed.
- Recognition is the most powerful tool you have to improve individual and work-group performance.
- A positive work environment is characterized as four positive "strokes" (recognition of good performance) for each negative stroke (correction).

APPLICATION EXERCISE

Figure 4-7 provides a way to analyze how enriched the job is for one of your employees. Complete the form by rating each core dimension of the employee's job on a scale from 1 to 5. Then indicate what you will do to enrich that job by changing one or more of the core dimensions. (For a larger version of this and the other application exercise forms, visit www.aboutiwp.com.)

FIGURE 4-7. JOB-ENRICHMENT EXERCISE

Job-Enrichment Assessment and Planned Changes

Core Dimensions	Rating: Low				High
task identity: Employees can identify with the final product	1	2	3	4	5
task significance: Employees can see the relationship between their work and the final product	1	2	3	4	5
variety of skills: Employees use many skills to complete their work	1	2	3	4	5
autonomy: Employees make decisions regarding how the work process is done	1	2	3	4	5
feedback: Employees receive timely, specific feedback on the work they have done	1	2	3	4	5
responsibility: Employees are given responsibility for the completion of the tasks	1	2	3	4	5

How will you make changes to enrich this job?

task identity: ____________________

____

____

task significance: ____________________

____

____

(continues)

FIGURE 4-7. CONTINUED

variety of skills: ______________________________

____

____

autonomy: ______________________________

____

____

feedback: ______________________________

____

____

responsibility: ______________________________

____

____

Notes

1. Abraham Maslow, *Motivation and Personality*, 2nd ed. (New York: Harper and Row, 1970).
2. Frederick Herzberg, *Work and the Nature of Man* (Cleveland, Ohio: World Publishing, 1966).
3. Richard Hackman, Greg Oldham, R. Janson, and K. Purdy, "A New Strategy for Job Enrichment," *California Management Review* 17, no. 4 (1975): 57–71.

"The way a team plays as a whole determines its success. You may have the greatest bunch of individual stars in the world, but if they don't play together, the club won't be worth a dime."

—BABE RUTH

CHAPTER 5

Developing Teamwork

A high-performing workgroup is more than just a group of high-performing individuals; it is a group of individuals who function well together. There are three main components to the task of building a high-performing team: *selection in* of the right people who make up the team, *development* of the players as individuals and as a team, and *selection out* of those who do not perform at the expected level. If you can't accomplish all three, your chances for building a high-performing team are nil.

This chapter examines the nature of groups and how they perform, then applies those observations to the task of team-building. It is not enough for you to work within the formal structure that your organization provides. You must go further and identify how the informal groups and leaders impact performance.

Formal vs. Informal Group Structures

There is a lot a manager can learn about building high-performing teams by studying the composition and action of people in groups. A *group* is defined as two or more people interacting for a common goal. Groups can have either a formal or an informal structure. In business, formal groups are designated by organizations using terms like *division, branch, department*, and *section*. These groups have formal leaders who have been designated to lead the people assigned to their respective units. Policies and regulations are developed to guide the work process.

But within this formal structure, there is an informal structure that also controls performance and can bypass the formal organizational boundaries. These latter groups are formed by various individuals who have common needs and desires; for example, to take care of the employees' security and social needs. Informal leaders emerge as well, empowered by the members of the informal group. The informal group also forms *norms*—expected patterns of behavior that the group members have for each other. The larger the formal organization, the more informal groups will exist.

Within all groups, there can be tension between the formal and informal structure and leadership. Policies and standards may not be the same as expectations, for example. The better the formal and informal structures are aligned, the better the performance of the team. As a manager, you should be aware of the informal groups within your formal group. It is through the informal group structure that you can be especially effective in building a winning team.

The Dynamics of the Informal Group

Informal groups form as employees seek to satisfy needs that are not otherwise being satisfied in the work environment. While, from the organization's point of view, the purpose of employment is to have employees work to accomplish the organization's goals, employees have psychological and social needs that they want to satisfy on the job. To satisfy these needs, employees often seek out others in the workgroup with similar needs and then form informal groups that can impact performance.

Perhaps the most important of these employee needs that is satisfied by an informal group is that of social needs. (See Chapter 4 for Maslow's hierarchy of needs.)

Employees with strong social needs will want to satisfy that need by being with others who also have that strong social need. And the more they want to be members of such an informal group, the more readily they will accept the work standards set by that group.

As mentioned earlier, another reason employees seek an informal group is to satisfy their security needs. The underlying idea is that there is safety in numbers: employees believe that the group can make a better defense against management, that the group offers some protection from management's decisions that might harm them.

Lastly, informal groups give their members an opportunity for leadership, which satisfies the need for self-esteem. If the work these employees do is not rewarding, providing them with an opportunity to satisfy their higher-level needs, leadership of an informal group is a very attractive alternative.

These leaders of informal groups are empowered by their members because of their personalities, competence, interpersonal skills, and integrity. They can be identified as the people others go to with their professional and personal problems. They are sought out because of their experience and willingness to share that experience, or because of their willingness to listen, and assurances of confidentiality.

Informal group leaders can be a valuable resource for a manager, as long as they do not become a substitute manager. The closer the goals of the informal leaders are aligned with those of the formal organization, the more productive the group will be.

Group Norms, for Good and Bad Results

The most powerful force influencing productivity and overall performance is group norms. The group can exert tremendous pressure on anyone who does not conform to these expectations, as can be seen when society's norms are violated. But how does a manager discover the norms of an informal group in his or her workgroup? Norms can best be seen in the behavior of the leaders of the informal group, who shape the behavior for the members of that group.

Group norms can form quickly and can have either a positive or a negative impact on performance. If group norms exceed the organization's standards, high performance is ensured. But if the norms are less than the organization's standards, the desired level of performance will be inhibited. How does this play out in a typical setting?

I encountered an example of a group norm when I was forming a workgroup with seven individuals assigned as instructors for a newly established U.S. Coast Guard leadership school. The norms for work habits developed quickly and included when to start the workday. The regulation stated that instructors had to be in their assigned workspace, ready to work, by 7:30 A.M. I would arrive at 7:25 A.M. each day, and I noticed that the coffee was already made and that my staff had already discussed what work was to be done that day. This was a good norm, as it was better than the standard.

So, as the formal leader of this workgroup, I decided to go in the same time as they did: 7:15 A.M. To my surprise, the instructors started to come in at about 7:00 A.M. It was then that I learned that the norm wasn't to be in fifteen minutes before the regulation start time, but to be in fifteen minutes before I arrived. I decided to try an experiment. I slowly moved my arrival time back a few minutes each day, and this was countered by my staff's arriving earlier and earlier. By the time I got to coming in at 6:30 A.M., I had become too predictable. When I arrived at 6:30, no one was there and no one showed up until exactly 7:30. We talked through the concept of norms, and we all now had a great example to use in class. I went back to coming in at 7:25, and they went back to coming in at 7:10.

Then one morning, one of my staff showed up in the parking lot the same time as I did. As the formal leader, I didn't think he was late. But when he entered the building, he was greeted by a barrage of comments, the nicest of which was, "Hey, Barry, did you sleep in this morning?" He wasn't late by the regulations, but he was definitely late by the norms set by the group.

Later in the day, Barry said to me, "You know, if I'm going to be late again," using his fingers to indicate quotes around the word *late*, "I'm not coming in until 9:30 so that all the grief I get will be worth it."

I replied, "Think again; then, the grief would come from me for anything after 7:30."

Norms form quickly and control such things as start times, length of breaks, and appearance. They can impact performance in terms of quantity, quality, time, and cost. Informal group norms often dictate more about performance than formal standards do, both positively and negatively. If your employees are not meeting the level of performance set by your work standards, there's probably a problem with the workgroup's unofficial norms.

As a manager, you have been designated by your organization as the formal leader for your workgroup. You are responsible for ensuring that the organization's policies and regulations as well as work standards are followed by the people in your workgroup. If you earn their confidence, you can also become an informal leader whom they will seek out for answers to personal and/or professional problems. This will give you greater power to shape the norms of your workgroup and align them with the policies and procedures of the organization.

In summary, many managers believe that performance is most influenced by the formal organization, with its designated leaders and written policies and procedures that set the standards for employee performance. In reality, the informal groups within the organization, with their informal leaders and informal group norms, are often the real determinants of workgroup performance. Thus, organizations are more productive when the formal and informal structures are aligned, as shown in Figure 5-1. As the earlier Coast Guard example shows, when informal norms for performance are the same as or higher than organizational standards, employees will meet or exceed the standards for productivity and quality. But if informal norms are lower than organizational standards, performance will fall short of expectations.

Introducing New Employees to Group Norms

Some organizations invest more than others in shaping the performance of their new employees. In one organization, the best employees were given responsibility for working with new employees, acting as informal mentors and showing them

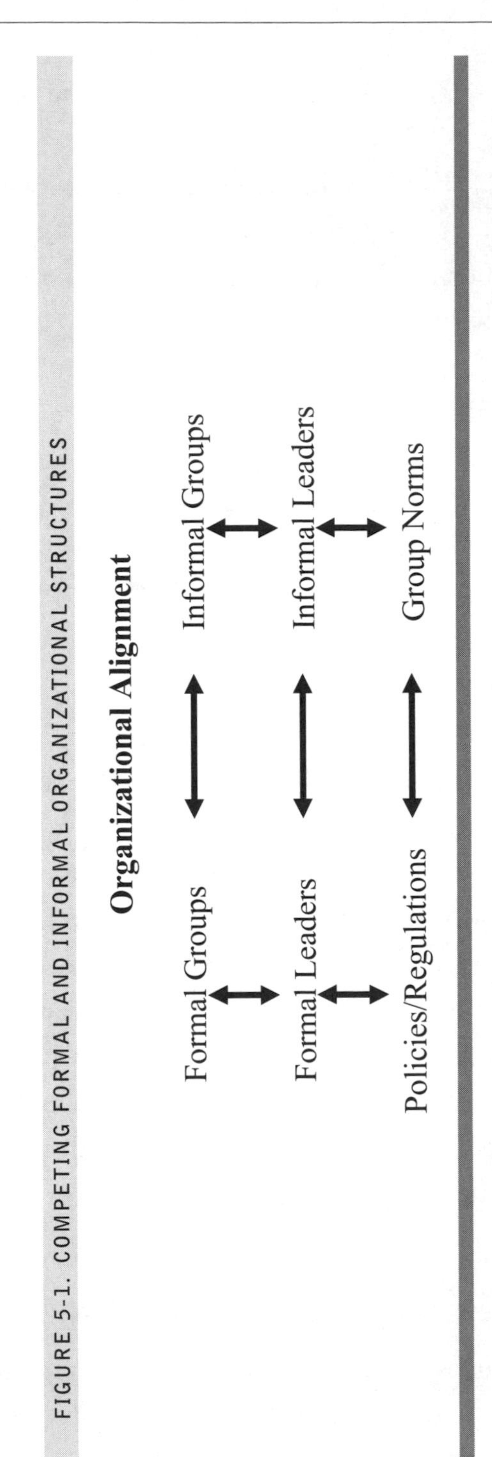

FIGURE 5-1. COMPETING FORMAL AND INFORMAL ORGANIZATIONAL STRUCTURES

how to do their jobs. These top-performing employees were given extra money to take new employees to lunch each day and as rewards for assuming this additional role.

In providing this type of training, the company exposed its new employees to the best way to do the work and gave them mentors whom they could go to with problems as they learned their jobs. The organization reinforced the roles of the informal group leaders and inculcated new employees in group norms that were aligned with organizational standards for performance.

Contrast this situation to the way in which many organizations handle their new employees. Very often the newcomers are left on their own to learn the ropes. Orientation programs tell them what's expected, but they quickly learn to ask, "How do we *really* do it?" Informal group leaders, whose attitudes might not be aligned with organizational standards, are happy to promote group norms by shaping the performance of the new employees the way they see fit. Wouldn't you rather have the former situation than the latter in your organization?

Changing Undesirable Group Norms

Managers need to identify the informal groups that make up their workgroups, find the informal leaders within those workgroups, and examine their norms for workplace performance. If those norms meet or exceed the organization's standards for performance, they should be continued and encouraged. However, if the norms are counterproductive, a manager needs to work to change them.

The first step in this process is to determine what the group norms are and determine their impact on performance. Observe the group as it works, and discuss its performance with the informal leaders or with the whole workgroup. The second step is to raise awareness of the informal leader's role and the existence of group norms, as well as their impact on performance. Then, the third step is to give the group an opportunity to suggest alternatives to do the work more efficiently. An informal group will not change its norms for behavior until the members of the group are aware of their existence and recognize their impact on performance. The last step is to reinforce movement toward the desired performance level.

Team Building—The Manager's Chief Task

A key factor in your success as a manager is how well you can build a strong team. As mentioned earlier in the chapter, the three most important factors in team building are selection of the team, training and development, and removal of undesirable members. Other key elements for building a high-performing team include:

- Development of clear expectations, including a vision and a course of action that all members understand
- Team participation in planning so as to gain commitment of the team members
- Identification of performance gaps, or the difference between the present and the desired levels of performance, and performance inhibitors, or those factors that will limit performance
- Acceptance of and commitment by team members to what will be done and how progress will be measured
- Fair assignment of roles and responsibilities to team members

Since involving the team members in some of the decision making is critical, this process goes through four distinct stages:[1]

1. *Forming*: The polite exchanges between team members as they begin to work together.
2. *Storming*: The more intense interactions as members let each other know their positions on the issues at hand.
3. *Norming*: The development of trust and norms for how the group will interact and work together.
4. *Performing*: The efficient work together as a group with shared goals.

One of the key factors throughout the four stages of team building is that of establishing trust—trust for the leader and trust for each other. Without trust, members of the group will typically stay in the storming stage, where individual agendas prevail.

Process vs. Content

A manager needs to understand what is happening within the group. Is there a problem preventing further movement toward the goal? Are there difficulties in how the work is shared? You will meet with the group and listen to what is being said, but you need to do more than simply hear the content of what is being discussed; you need to also observe the process—how the group is interacting. *Content* is what is being done or being talked about. *Process* is how the individuals are relating to one another.

Learn to observe the process while being involved in the content of what is being said. Consider having another formal leader, or possibly an informal leader, run the meeting so that you can observe the group process, getting involved in the content only when necessary.

Observation of the process will reveal three different behavioral patterns within any group:

1. *Task behavior* is directed toward getting the job done. This may involve giving directions, initiating procedures, setting standards, giving or seeking information, clarifying, or summarizing. Task behavior may be shown by any member of the group, but it usually is associated with the formal and informal leaders.

2. *Relationship or maintenance behavior* is directed toward maintaining the group as a unit by supporting, encouraging, relieving tension, actively listening, or seeking compromises. Relationship behavior may also be shown by informal leaders or any other member of the group.

3. *Personal behavior* is when individuals attempt to satisfy their needs without concern for the goals of the group. This may include seeking recognition, withdrawing, blocking, attacking, or repeatedly changing topics.

The formal leader of the group (presumably you, as manager) ensures that there is enough task behavior to accomplish the goals of the organization, enough relationship behavior to maintain the group as a tight unit, and enough constructive outlets for personal behavior. Other formal leaders or informal leaders may be allowed to lead within the group, with the senior formal leader observing the group, giving direction and support only when necessary.

Group Decision Making

With greater use of participative management techniques, there has been an increase in the use of groups to analyze and make decisions within organizations. While there are advantages, group decision making has many potential problems as well. For example, the advantages, or reasons for involving groups in the decision-making process, include:

- The group discussion provides a better analysis of the problem because of the different backgrounds and motives of the group members.
- Suggestions may come from individuals closer to the problem.
- The discussion may give rise to ideas that leaders would not have had on their own.
- Individuals in the group will have ownership of, and greater commitment to, the decision because they participated in the process.
- Individuals in the group are shielded from personal liability or criticism for the decision.

The disadvantages are more subtle but must also be considered:

- Greater time and personnel are necessary.
- The solutions generated for the group might not align with the organization's goals.

- The group may have a tendency to take greater risks since there is no individual accountability for the decision.
- One individual or an informal group leader may dominate the decision-making process.
- The power of the leader or the organizational climate may keep members from expressing their true opinions.
- If the decision is not accepted by management, the process may aggravate an already unacceptable situation.

As a formal leader, you are responsible for the performance of your workgroup. To build a high-performing team, you will need to work within the existing informal structure, leadership, and norms to improve and/or maintain performance.

Tips on Team Building

Your role as a manager is to develop your workgroups into high-performing teams. When doing so, bear the following in mind:

- Organizations are more productive when the formal and informal structures are aligned, in that the formal leader is also an informal leader and uses other informal group leaders appropriately; and in that the norms of the group align with the organization's regulations. Your role as a manager is to ensure that this alignment takes place.
- Your role as a formal leader is to ensure that there is enough task behavior (direction) to ensure that the work is done, enough maintenance behavior (support) to keep the workgroup functioning as a team, and enough outlets for personal behavior.
- As you lead your workgroup, be involved in the content of what is being discussed while also observing the process of how it is being done.
- Allow informal leaders to give needed task and maintenance behavior, freeing you to observe the process of the group.

- Know the stage your workgroup is at, as your leadership will need to adjust accordingly, whether forming, storming, norming, or performing.
- The three most important tasks in building a high-performing team are selection in, training and development, and selection out.
- Use members of your workgroup to gain commitment to a course of action, but remember that it requires more time and can lead to unacceptable recommendations if they don't know all the constraints.

APPLICATION EXERCISE

Identify the informal groups that make up your workgroup. Who are the informal leaders within each group? What norms exist within each group, and how do they impact performance? Use the format outlined in Figure 5-2 to analyze your workgroup. (For a larger version of this and the other application exercise forms, visit www.aboutiwp.com.)

FIGURE 5-2. ANALYZING INFORMAL GROUPS EXERCISE

Informal Group A:

Members: ______

Informal Leaders: ______

Norms: ______

How will you improve performance? ______

Informal Group B:

Members: ______

Informal Leaders: ______

Norms: ______

How will you improve performance? ______

Note

1. Bruce Tuckman, "Developmental Sequence in Small Groups," *Psychological Bulletin* 63: 384–99.

SECTION 2

Identifying and Removing Barriers to Performance

"I can't improve it if I can't measure it."

—WILLIAM THOMSON, LORD KELVIN

CHAPTER 6

Defining the Performance Gap

The act of measurement is critical to improving performance of your employees. Lord Kelvin's quote above dates from 1906 and applies today as much as it did 100 years ago. Jack Welch, the former CEO of General Electric, described the importance of measurement at a conference I attended in 2001 as "You get what you measure." And the comment struck home, because I have believed in the importance of performance measurement since 1977, when I first used the phrase, "What gets measured gets done."[1]

In this chapter we take a look at performance measurement—how to measure existing performance, set measurable goals, and close the gap between the present and desired levels of performance.

Establishing a Baseline Performance Level

Before a manager can discuss a performance shortfall or gap with under-performing employees, there has to be a clearly defined level of performance, expressed in measurable terms, that will establish a baseline for future comparison. Measures for quantity or productivity are very often such starting points. But productivity measures alone do not give a clear picture of employees' present levels of performance.

Businesses need a measurable way to gauge productivity. In manufacturing, performance may be described as the number of units produced, the rate of rejection by Quality Assurance, or the number of calls on warranty. Or it may be measured as the cost of production and/or the amount of waste produced, or the time it takes to produce each unit. Stated differently, performance can be defined by measures for productivity (quantity), quality, time, and cost. An example from sales is to tally the number of units sold and/or the revenue produced, or the mix of products sold, the cost of each sale, and the timeframe for the sale.

Once you have measured where you are (the present level of performance), the next step is to describe where you'd like to be (the desired level of performance). Here again, it is necessary to identify the desired level of performance in measurable terms. The difference between where you are and where you want to be is called the *performance gap*, as shown in Figure 6-1.

Analyzing the Performance Gap and Setting a Reasonable Goal

Once the gap in performance has been identified, the next step is to set a *reasonable goal* that can be met in a short time, such as three months to a year. The reasonable goal is a milestone, an interim goal, that, when met, will indicate progress in closing the performance gap, as shown in Figure 6-2. The reasonable goal should be described using the same measures of quantity, quality, time, and cost as used for the baseline analysis.

The reason for setting a reasonable goal is to give the employees a target that can be met in short order and relatively easily, and which, when met, will provide the motivation to continue meeting higher goals. Very often, when the desired level of performance is too far from the present level of performance, the goal appears impossible to reach. Performance is often improved one step at a time, and the reasonable goal is a way of communicating that first step to your employees.

FIGURE 6-1. DEFINING THE PERFORMANCE GAP

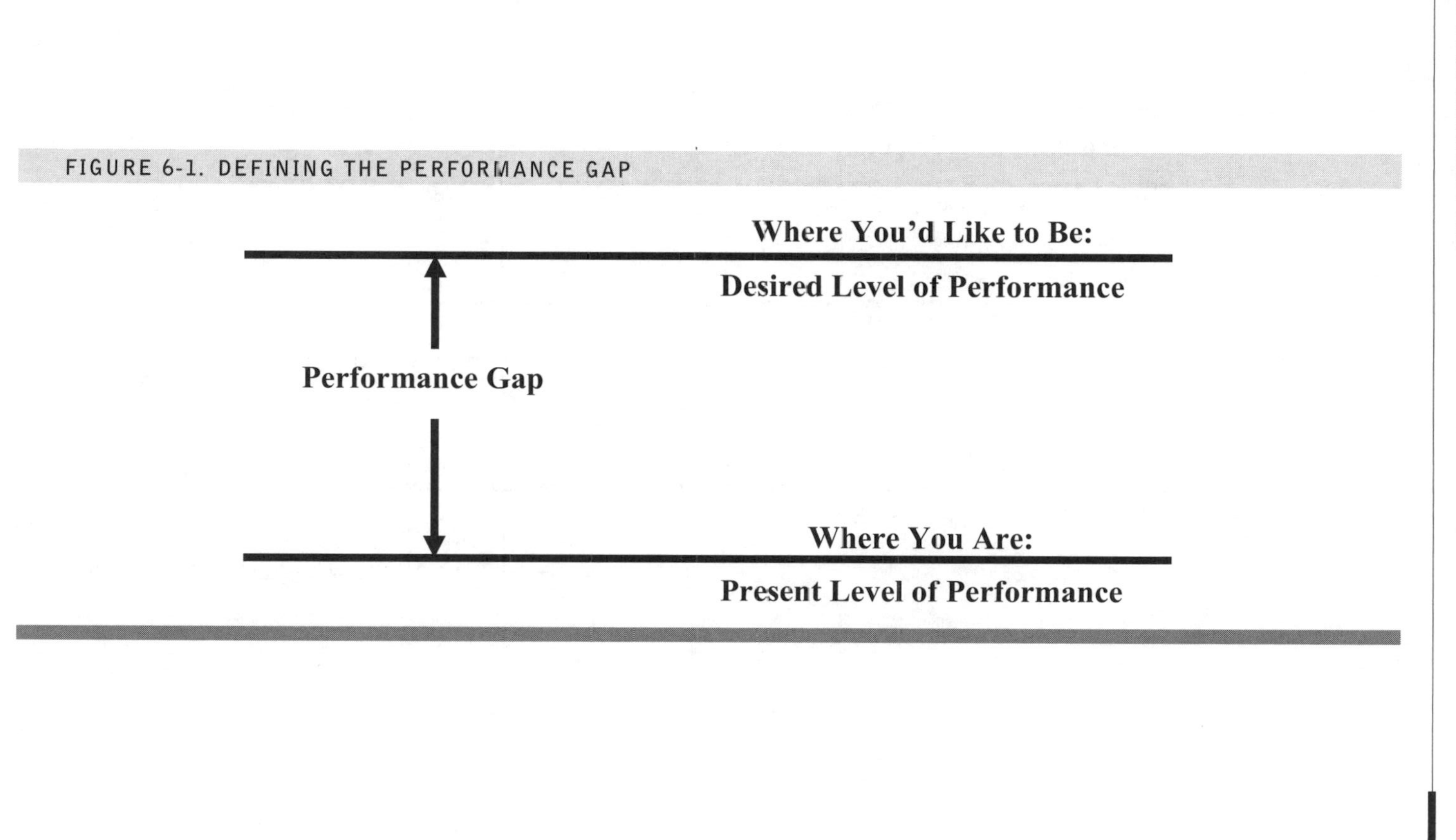

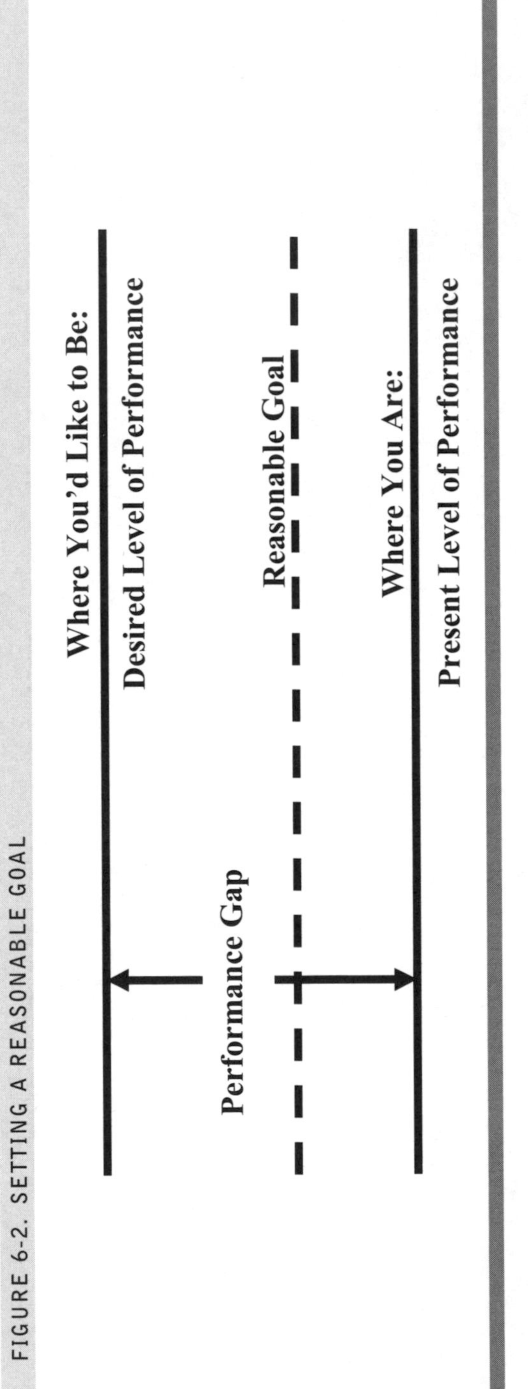

FIGURE 6-2. SETTING A REASONABLE GOAL

Ultimately, to determine whether you are successful in closing a performance gap, you will need to identify the factors working for you (driving forces) and the factors working against you (restraining forces). Figure 6-3 depicts the forces working for and against closing the performance gap. Notice that these forces are shown with different lengths, depicting their relative strengths. The longer the line, the greater the impact on closing the performance gap. Chapter 7 details how to identify these forces, but for now you should just be aware of their existence.

This analysis gives a "snapshot in time" of the present level of performance, the desired level of performance, the reasonable goal, and the forces working for and against you as you try to close the performance gap.

Gathering Information from Employees

To gather the information you need in order to establish the present and desired levels of performance and to examine the reasons for any performance gaps, you will need to ask your employees the right questions, in the right order. Your goals are to clarify the situation, to identify the performance gaps, and to determine the causes before you develop strategies to improve performance. Of course, involving them in the process will give them greater ownership of the results, and you'll get a greater commitment to improving performance.

While your questions may be prepared in a logical order, the actual flow of conversation may move back and forth among these three types of questions:

1. *Situation questions*: You begin with open-ended questions to assess the overall situation and gather background information. If you have done your homework, you can limit the questions to a few basic ones. Unfortunately, many new managers spend too much time asking too many open-ended questions, usually to make up for their lack of preparation. Examples of open-ended situation questions are: "How have things been going on the job?" and "What problems or challenges are you experiencing on the job?"

FIGURE 6-3. IDENTIFYING DRIVING AND RESTRAINING FORCES

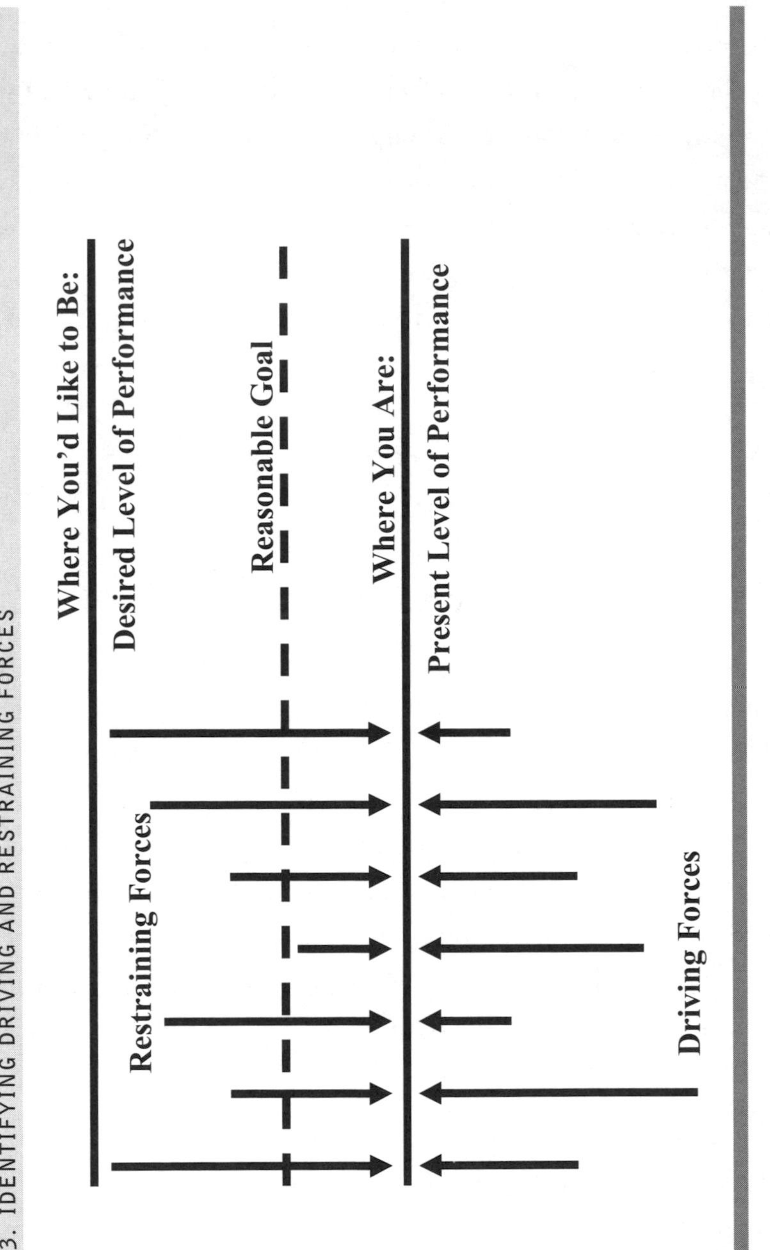

2. *Performance gap questions*: You build on what you have learned by following up with direct questions to determine the difference between the present performance (where you are) and desired performance (where you'd like to be). You also determine how your employees presently measure their performance and how they would close the performance gap. Examples of performance-gap questions are: "How would you describe your present level of performance?" "Given your present level of performance, what is the desired level of performance?" "How will we determine whether you've closed the gap between where you are and where you'd like to be?"

3. *Cause/opportunity questions*: While your employees may not completely understand the performance gap and its causes, you must gain their perceptions. Begin by asking about the work environment and follow with questions about how the employee is performing the tasks. Examples of cause/opportunity questions are: "What factors from the work environment are contributing to the performance shortfall?" "Do you have a clear understanding of what's expected?" "Do you receive enough feedback on your performance?" "Do you have the tools, time, and other resources you need?"

Conducting a Performance-Assessment Meeting

Develop an agenda for a meeting with employees that follows a pattern of describing and getting feedback on present and desired levels of performance, on setting reasonable goals for improving performance, and on identifying the driving and restraining forces on closing the performance gap.

Think about who should attend the meeting, making sure that you have selected formal and informal leaders of your workgroup. The meeting should be limited to about six people, so as to get a good mix of ideas while having a group that is manageable. Then pick a time and place for the meeting and inform the participants of the agenda.

Begin the meeting by discussing the present and desired levels of performance and get feedback from participants as to how they perceive the difference. Then solicit ideas on what would constitute a reasonable goal, and be sure it is expressed in terms of measurable changes. Remember that you want the participants' involvement in the goal-setting and measurement process so that they will be committed to reaching those goals.

Performance Coaching for Goal Achievement

Does this pattern of questioning sound familiar? Chapter 3 presented the Performance Counseling Guide as a tool for assessing follower readiness (see Figure 3-4). This guide can also be used for conducting a performance-gap analysis with your workgroup. Figure 6-4 shows how the questions you ask regarding any performance gap fit with the Performance Counseling Guide.

Tips for Defining the Performance Gap

Here are some tips to help measure performance—as it exists and as you would like it to be.

- Establishing a clearly defined performance gap is the first step in improving performance.
- The starting point for identifying the performance gap is to describe the present level of performance (where you are) in measurable terms (quantity, quality, time, and cost where possible).
- The next step is to describe the desired level of performance (where you'd like to be) in measurable terms.
- The final step is to set a reasonable goal that can be met easily and that will offer the promise of closing the performance gap in the near future.
- Involve some of your people in the performance analysis so that they will buy into the problem and its causes and be committed to the action that you jointly decide to take.

FIGURE 6-4. QUESTION-ASKING TECHNIQUES AND PERFORMANCE COUNSELING GUIDE

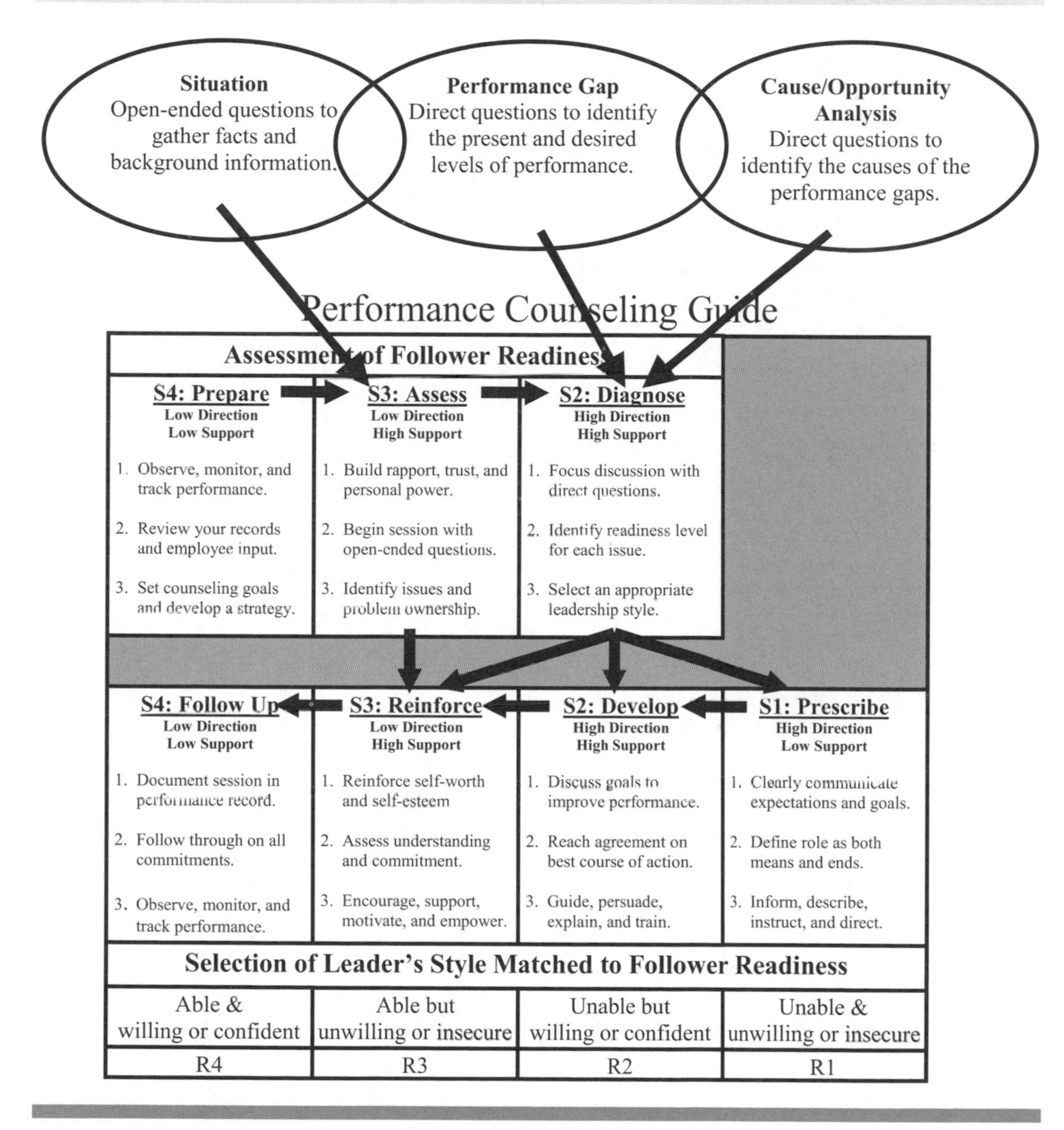

- Lead the discussion with your workgroup to identify the overall situation, identify the performance gap in measurable terms, and determine the causes and solutions (to be discussed in Chapters 7 and 8).

APPLICATION EXERCISE

Use Figure 6-5 to identify a performance gap that you currently face, set a reasonable goal, and determine how you will measure results. (For a larger version of this and the other application exercise forms, visit www.aboutiwp.com.)

FIGURE 6-5. GAP-ANALYSIS EXERCISE

Gap-Analysis Worksheet

Present Level of Performance: ______________________________

____

____

____

Desired Level of Performance: ______________________________

____

____

____

Reasonable Goal: ______________________________

____

____

____

Remember that you should describe these with measures of quantity, quality, time, and cost if possible.

What measurement is already being done by your organization to track this performance? What measures are appropriate to track as you work to close the performance gap you have described above?

____

____

____

____

____

____

____

____

Note

1. Roger Chevalier, "Evaluation: The Link Between Learning and Performance," *Performance Improvement* 43, no. 4 (2004): 40–44.

"If you pit a good performer against a bad system, the system will win almost every time."

—GEARY RUMMLER AND ALAN BRACHE

CHAPTER 7

Identifying the Causes of Performance Problems

Research has shown that about 85 percent of performance problems are related to the work environment while only 15 percent are related to the individual.[1] Yet many managers spend most of their time trying to "fix their employees," when it's the work environment that needs to be fixed.

Before deciding on a solution to remedy a performance shortfall, you should do a systematic assessment of the possible causes. Then you will be in a better position to choose the best solution to improve your employees' workplace performance. This chapter provides a way to analyze the many factors that can negatively affect performance.

Is It the Environment or Is It the Individual?

The *work environment* consists of three elements that you as a manager must ensure are correct if your people are to perform their jobs properly: information, resources, and incentives. That is, the work environment that you create should include adequate information to guide them, the necessary resources to do the job, and the proper incentives for doing the job right.

The *individual* must have a corresponding three elements: knowledge, capacity, and motives. That is, the person must have the knowledge and skills to do the job, the capacity to learn and do the job, and the right motives for doing the job and remaining in the organization (see Figure 7-1).[2] Keep in mind that your job is to create a work environment where your employees can succeed, but this will only happen if you have the right people.

Attention to the Environment

Let's begin the examination of performance problems with a look at the three elements that constitute work environment.

Information

The most important means for improving employee performance is to provide clear expectations. This starts with giving an up-to-date job description that is reinforced every day by the comments you make. The performance-coaching cycle described in Chapter 1 begins with this process, as you focus on both the means (the activities needed to be successful) and the ends (the desired outcome of their work).

The next steps, which are repeated again and again in the performance-coaching cycle, are observing performance, providing timely and specific feedback, recording examples of the employee's work, and adjusting goals as necessary. These activities are necessary to shape the performance of your employees through the feedback you provide, which helps to clarify and reinforce your expectations.

Another critical aspect of information is a relevant guide or job aid that provides additional direction when needed. This can come in the form of a checklist, diagram, or flowchart that provides a systematic approach to completing work that is done infrequently or needs to be done with a high degree of accuracy.

Leadership and counseling, as described in Chapters 2 and 3, are necessary to

FIGURE 7-1. IMPACT OF WORK ENVIRONMENT AND INDIVIDUAL ON PERFORMANCE

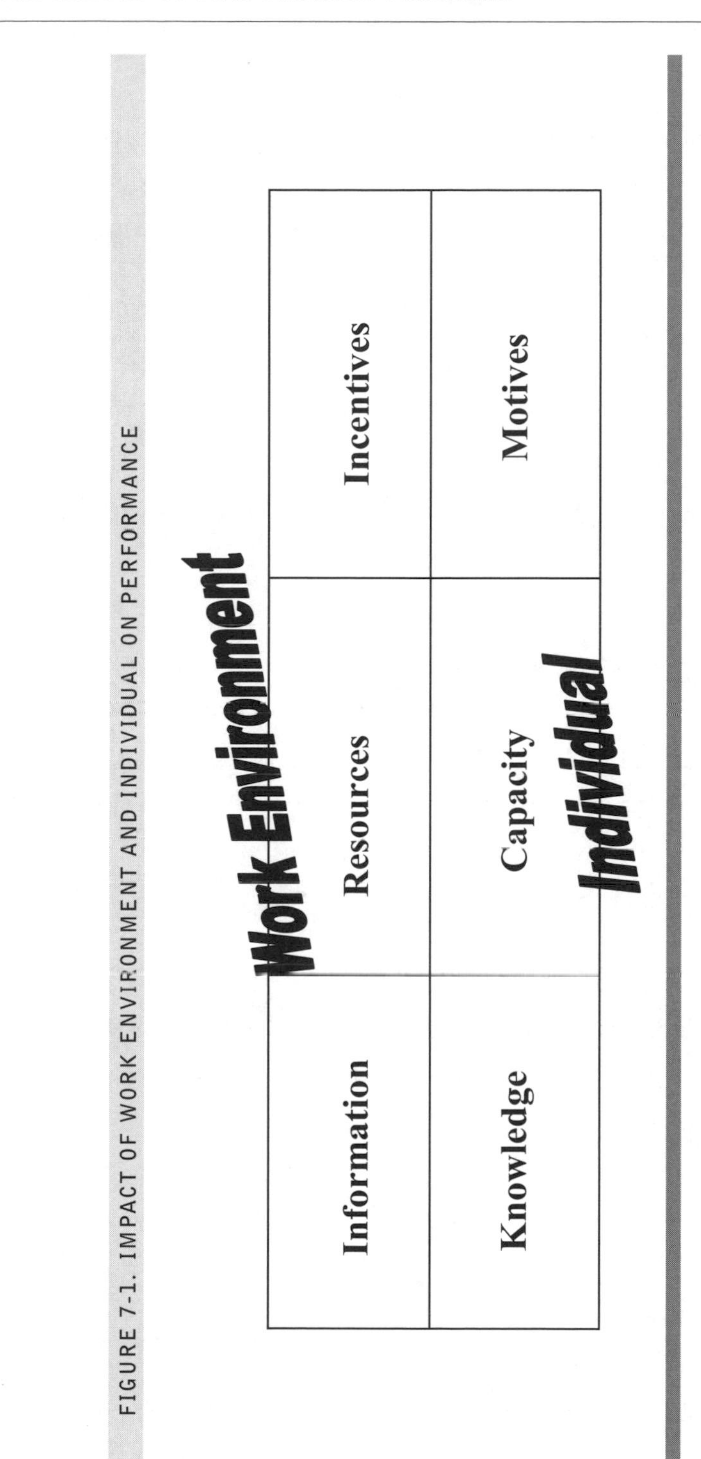

create this part of the work environment. As mentioned earlier, you must adjust your leadership style and the amount of direction and support you give to match your employees' readiness (ability and willingness) for their tasks. You must also provide counseling as a way of offering feedback and direction as necessary. In summary:

1. Roles and performance expectations are clearly defined; employees are given relevant and frequent feedback about the adequacy of performance.
2. Clear and relevant guides are used to describe the work process.
3. Leadership and coaching guide employee performance and development.

Resources

Your employees need to have the right equipment and materials to do the job. They also need enough time to do the job right. They need the work processes and procedures clearly stated and in a standardized way so work is done correctly.

Resources also include a work environment that is both physically and psychologically safe, clean, and organized. Like the maintenance factors described in Chapter 4, this will not ensure the best performance, but its absence will limit the effectiveness of your employees. In summary:

1. Materials, tools, and time needed to do the job are present.
2. Processes and procedures are clearly defined and enhance individual performance if followed.
3. Overall physical and psychological work environment contributes to improved performance; work conditions are safe, clean, organized, and conducive to performance.

Incentives

It is with the incentives that you offer employees that measurement becomes critical, as was indicated in Chapter 6. Be sure that you have measures for quantity, quality, time, and cost, as all will impact performance. If you have measures for only quantity, then quality, time, and cost may be affected, as your employees strive to meet their numbers goal. Similarly, if you measure and set goals for only for quality, then quantity, time, and cost will likely go out the window.

But measurement itself is not enough to ensure high performance. Some form of reinforcement is necessary. While you want to have positive consequences for good work and negative consequences for poor work, this is not always the case. For example, when a manager gives top performers more work to do since they get it done so well, the employees often perceive this as being punishment for doing good work. The reverse can happen as well, as when a manager takes away work from an underperforming employee, thus rewarding poor performance. Figure 7-2 shows the consequences and outcomes of differing performance.

The most fundamental incentive is positive feedback for good performance. The feedback should be timely and specific. Financial incentives, such as pay raises and/or bonuses, can be used to reward exceptional performance. Nonfinancial rewards can also be used to reward performance; no one does this better than the military, where medals are routinely used to reward performance. Many organizations have special gifts with the company logo that can only be received for exceptional performance. I still have the gold Cross pen with the Century 21 logo on my desk as a reminder of the recognition I was given when working for that company.

As was discussed in Chapter 4, job enrichment can be a powerful incentive. Jobs for which employees have a sense of accomplishment, are learning and using new skills, and have greater responsibility will motivate top performers to continue delivering exceptional work. The overall work environment should be positive, one in which employees believe that each challenge is an opportunity to succeed and there are regular opportunities for advancement. All too often, the work environment can best be described as "management by exception," where managers focus only on what has gone wrong. In summary:

1. Measurement and reward systems reinforce positive performance; financial and nonfinancial incentives are present.

FIGURE 7-2. JOB PERFORMANCE AND ITS CONSEQUENCES AND OUTCOMES

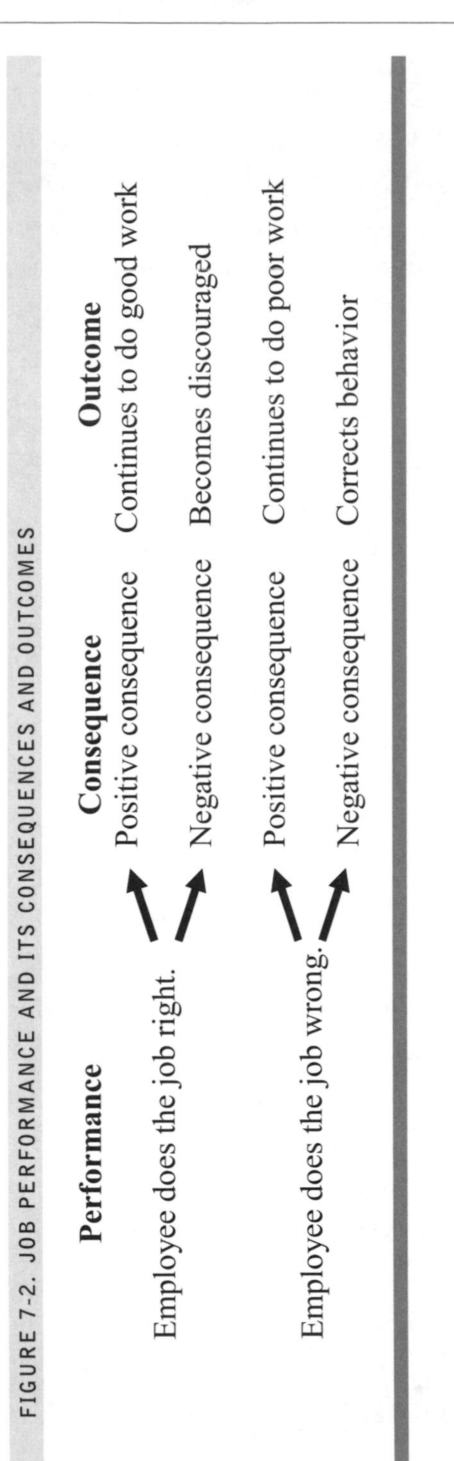

2. Jobs are enriched to allow for fulfillment of employee needs.
3. Overall work environment is positive, where employees believe they have an opportunity to succeed; career development opportunities are present. Any of the factors listed under the headings of Information, Resources, and Incentives in Figure 7-3 can impact performance.

Attention to the Individual

While the work environment has many important factors that must be right to produce sustained performance, you also need to have the right people. As mentioned earlier in the book, selection is one of the keys to building a high-performing team. If you start with the wrong people, you may never be able to get the results that you need.

Selection should focus on employees' knowledge and skills, capacity to learn, and motives for working. Let's look at each of these factors.

FIGURE 7-3. INFORMATION, RESOURCES, AND INCENTIVES THAT INFLUENCE PERFORMANCE

Work Environment

Information	Resources	Incentives
1. Roles and performance expectations are clearly defined; employees are given relevant and frequent feedback about the adequacy of performance. 2. Clear and relevant guides are used to describe the work process. 3. Leadership and coaching guide employee performance and development.	1. Materials, tools, and time needed to do the job are present. 2. Processes and procedures are clearly defined and enhance individual performance if followed. 3. Overall physical and psychological work environment contributes to improved performance; work conditions are safe, clean, organized, and conducive to performance.	1. Measurement and reward systems reinforce positive performance; financial and nonfinancial incentives are present. 2. Jobs are enriched to allow for fulfillment of employee needs. 3. Overall work environment is positive, where employees believe they have an opportunity to succeed; career-development opportunities are present.

Knowledge and Skills

While many managers believe that selecting employees with the requisite knowledge and skill is the starting point for improving group performance, it is often the most expensive and least effective way of doing so. You want to select employees with the necessary knowledge and skills, of course, but you also must be prepared to train and develop new members of your team. Additionally, you must properly place each member of the team based on the knowledge and skills that the individual has.

All members of your team do not have to have the same knowledge and skills. Just as with an athletic team, there are different positions that require different abilities. While it is good for each team member to understand the others' roles, they do not need to know how to do those jobs. You may, however, wish to cross-train the team so that you have greater flexibility in assigning tasks; this will also allow employees to learn and use a greater variety of skills. In summary:

1. Employees have the necessary knowledge, experience, and skills to do the desired behaviors.
2. Employees with the necessary knowledge, experience, and skills are properly placed to use and share what they know.
3. Employees are cross-trained to understand each other's roles.

Capacity

Employees should also be selected on the basis of their capacity to learn and do. All too often, organizations try to make up for poor selection with additional training. If you select the wrong people, you will spend a lot of time and money trying to train them. Another element of selection for capacity is to hire people who are free of emotional limitations for doing the job, such as salespeople who enjoy speaking with people or roofers who aren't afraid of heights.

For example, suppose you are a consultant for a major department store with a reputation for outstanding customer service. After observing employees working with customers in the store, you ask, "How did you train your people to be so polite?"

"We didn't," the trainer replies. "We hired people whose parents taught them to be polite."

In summary:

1. Employees have the capacity to learn and do what is needed to perform successfully.
2. Employees are recruited and selected to match the realities of the work situation.
3. Employees are free of emotional limitations that would interfere with their performance.

Motives

Employees come with their own set of needs, as was discussed in Chapter 4. You will not be able to change those needs that underlie their motives for working. But you can be sure that your employees are selected properly so as to ensure that their motives match the realities of the work environment.

An important question to ask when interviewing potential members of your team is, "*Why* do you want to work in this organization?" This starts a communication about job expectations, both the applicant's and yours. Actually, your expectations are first stated in the job announcement and advertising, and they continue to be stated throughout the application and selection process. By communicating clear expectations about the job, you inform applicants so that they can make correct decisions about the position.

I was interviewing an individual for an important position, and after I informed the applicant of the job requirements, he said, "You know, I didn't realize all the job required. I'm not sure that I really want the job anymore." My response was, "Thank you for your comment. We just saved each other from several unhappy years together."

In summary:

1. Motives of employees are aligned with the work and the work environment.
2. Employees desire to perform the required jobs.
3. Employees are recruited and selected to match the realities of the work situation.

Any of the individual factors for Knowledge and Skills, Capacity, and Motives, as shown in Figure 7-4, can also impact performance.

A Cause-Analysis Model

By combining the environmental and individual factors, you have a model for analyzing the causes of performance gaps,[3] as shown in Figure 7-5. This model can also be used to determine what needs to be done when creating a new work environment or a new team to respond to an existing environment.

FIGURE 7-4. KNOWLEDGE AND SKILLS, CAPACITY, AND MOTIVES THAT INFLUENCE PERFORMANCE

Individual

Knowledge/Skills	Capacity	Motives
1. Employees have the necessary knowledge, experience, and skills to do the desired behaviors.	1. Employees have the capacity to learn and do what is needed to perform successfully.	1. Motives of employees are aligned with the work and the work environment.
2. Employees with the necessary knowledge, experience, and skills are properly placed to use and share what they know.	2. Employees are recruited and selected to match the realities of the work situation.	2. Employees desire to perform the required jobs.
3. Employees are cross-trained to understand each other's roles.	3. Employees are free of emotional limitations that would interfere with their performance.	3. Employees are recruited and selected to match the realities of the work situation.

FIGURE 7-5. MODEL FOR ANALYZING POTENTIAL CAUSES OF PERFORMANCE GAPS

Cause Analysis Model

Work Environment

Information

1. Roles and performance expectations are clearly defined; employees are given relevant and frequent feedback about the adequacy of performance.
2. Clear and relevant guides are used to describe the work process.
3. Leadership and coaching guide employee performance and development.

Resources

1. Materials, tools, and time needed to do the job are present.
2. Processes and procedures are clearly defined and enhance individual performance if followed.
3. Overall physical and psychological work environment contributes to improved performance; work conditions are safe, clean, organized, and conducive to performance.

Incentives

1. Measurement and reward systems reinforce positive performance; financial and nonfinancial incentives are present.
2. Jobs are enriched to allow for fulfillment of employee needs.
3. Overall work environment is positive, where employees believe they have an opportunity to succeed; career-development opportunities are present.

Individual

Knowledge and Skills

1. Employees have the necessary knowledge, experience, and skills to do the desired behaviors.
2. Employees with the necessary knowledge, experience, and skills are properly placed to use and share what they know.
3. Employees are cross-trained to understand each other's roles.

Capacity

1. Employees have the capacity to learn and do what is needed to perform successfully.
2. Employees are recruited and selected to match the realities of the work situation.
3. Employees are free of emotional limitations that would interfere with their performance.

Motives

1. Motives of employees are aligned with the work and the work environment.
2. Employees desire to perform the required jobs.
3. Employees are recruited and selected to match the realities of the work situation.

Performance Analysis

Chapter 6 defined a performance gap as the difference between present and desired levels of performance, and there was information on how to set reasonable goals for performance improvement. There was also mention of the forces that work for or against employee improvement. Thus far in this chapter, there's been discussion of the environmental and individual factors that affect performance. The next step is to put this information together in a useful document to analyze performance.

The Performance Analysis Worksheet, depicted in Figure 7-7, provides a means for describing present and desired levels of performance and setting reasonable goals. On the left-hand side of the worksheet you will find the factors to evaluate in determining causes of a performance gap; these are the environmental and individual factors discussed earlier.

Performance Analysis Worksheet

Conducting a thorough cause analysis will help you to better define the reasons why a gap in performance exists. As described in Chapter 6, the starting point in using the Performance Analysis Worksheet is identifying the individual's or the organization's present level of performance (where you are) and their desired level of performance (where you'd like to be). The difference between the present and desired level of performance is the performance gap.

The next step is to communicate the performance gap to your formal and informal leaders and get feedback. The process continues in asking your employees questions to identify how each of these factors is presently impacting their performance gap. Force field analysis[4] provides a methodology for identifying and weighting the relative strength of the factors you have identified relating to performance. *Driving forces* are those factors that are already working to close the performance gap; these are evaluated as to relative strength on a scale from +1 to +4. *Restraining forces* are those factors working against closing the performance gap; these are evaluated as to relative strength on scale from -1 to -4. Figure 7-6 graphically depicts these opposing forces.

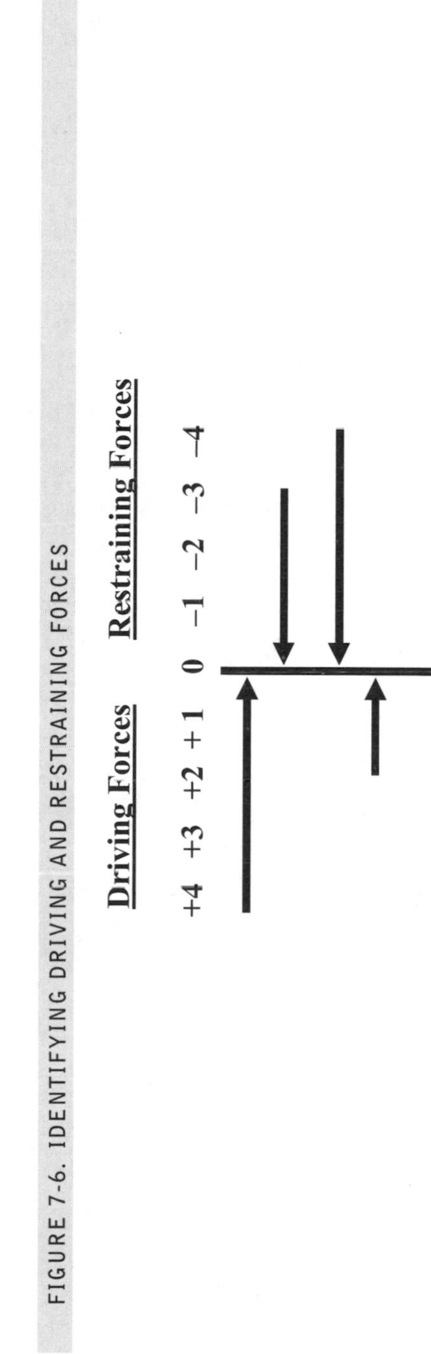

FIGURE 7-6. IDENTIFYING DRIVING AND RESTRAINING FORCES

Tips on Identifying the Causes of Performance Problems

Keep these tips in mind when you complete the Performance Analysis Worksheet.

- Eighty-five percent of performance shortfalls are caused by the work environment, whereas only 15 percent are caused by individuals.
- The work environment includes information (clear expectations, proper feedback, and coaching), resources (materials, equipment, time, clearly defined processes and procedures, and a safe work environment), and incentives (the right measures and rewards, enriched jobs, and career opportunities).
- Individuals should be selected based on their knowledge and skills, capacity to learn, and motives for seeking work.
- An analysis of the causes should be done before deciding on how to close the performance gap.
- The Performance Analysis Worksheet is a structure to analyze and display the performance gap and its causes.

APPLICATION EXERCISE

Using the Performance Analysis Worksheet (Figure 7-7), analyze the performance gap that you identified to complete the Application Exercise for Chapter 6. Do this analysis on your own, as Chapter 8 will describe how to repeat it with your workgroup. (For a larger version of this and the other application exercise forms, visit www.aboutiwp.com.)

FIGURE 7-7. PERFORMANCE ANALYSIS WORKSHEET FOR PERFORMANCE ANALYSIS EXERCISE

Present Level of Performance: ______________________________

____

Desired Level of Performance: ______________________________

____

Reasonable Goal: ______________________________

____

Factors	Driving Forces					Restraining Forces			
	+4	+3	+2	+1	0	−1	−2	−3	−4
Information									
clear expectations	.	.	.	.		.	.	.	.
relevant feedback	.	.	.	.		.	.	.	.
relevant guides	.	.	.	.		.	.	.	.
performance coaching	.	.	.	.		.	.	.	.
Resources									
materials/tools	.	.	.	.		.	.	.	.
time	.	.	.	.		.	.	.	.
clear processes/procedures	.	.	.	.		.	.	.	.
safe/organized environment	.	.	.	.		.	.	.	.
Incentives									
financial incentives	.	.	.	.		.	.	.	.
other incentives	.	.	.	.		.	.	.	.
enriched jobs	.	.	.	.		.	.	.	.
positive work environment	.	.	.	.		.	.	.	.
Motives									
motives aligned with work	.	.	.	.		.	.	.	.
employees desire to perform	.	.	.	.		.	.	.	.
expectations are realistic	.	.	.	.		.	.	.	.
recruit/select the right people	.	.	.	.		.	.	.	.

(continues)

FIGURE 7-7. CONTINUED

Factors	Driving Forces					Restraining Forces			
	+4	+3	+2	+1	0	−1	−2	−3	−4
Capacity									
capacity to learn	.	.	.	.		.	.	.	.
capacity to do what is needed	.	.	.	.		.	.	.	.
recruit/select the right people	.	.	.	.		.	.	.	.
emotional limitations	.	.	.	.		.	.	.	.
Knowledge/Skills									
required knowledge	.	.	.	.		.	.	.	.
required skills	.	.	.	.		.	.	.	.
placement	.	.	.	.		.	.	.	.
cross-trained	.	.	.	.		.	.	.	.

Notes

1. Geary Rummler and Alan Brache, *Improving Performance*, 2nd ed. (San Francisco: Jossey-Bass, 1995).
2. Thomas Gilbert, *Human Competence*, Tribute Edition (Washington, D.C.: International Society for Performance Improvement, 1988).
3. Roger Chevalier, "Updating the Behavioral Engineering Model," *Performance Improvement* 42, no. 5 (May/June 2003), 8–13.
4. Kurt Lewin, "Frontiers in Group Dynamics," *Human Relations*, vol. 1 (1947), 5–41.

"Why is it that we never have time to do it right, but we have time to do it again?"

—MARK TWAIN

CHAPTER 8

A Performance-Assessment Case Study

This chapter presents a case study of performance assessment in the area of sales. My role in this situation was that of a consultant working with the sales manager, but I have combined the roles so as to make the case study easier to follow. First, read the case study and define the performance gap. Then, you will be able to describe the reasonable goal and identify the driving and restraining forces using the Performance Analysis Worksheet. The suggested responses are provided later in the chapter, with explanation.

This case study is instructive because sales managers have a unique leadership challenge in that they do not see the vast majority of work done by their employees. While they sometimes accompany their salespeople on calls to prospective customers, the employees are not routinely observed, and without regular observation it is difficult for a sales manager to provide specific feedback.

The Case Study[1]

You have just been placed in charge of a new sales team; the former sales manager has left the job for health reasons. Your company has provided software products and services for large financial organizations and government agencies for the past eight years. The company recently decided to develop products and services for medium-sized financial institutions as well, and it formed a sales team to bring the new product to market. There has been only one sale to date, and that was made by your chief executive officer (CEO).

While the sales team is asking for additional training to enhance their skills, you would like to analyze the situation first to determine the underlying causes for the lack of success. Your immediate plan is to help develop the sales team while also establishing a relationship with Customer Service. While your long-term goal is to achieve three sales per salesperson each month within eighteen months, your short-term goal is one sale per salesperson per month within three months. The cost of the product is high, but it promises to make a customer's operations much smoother; also, your company will provide customer service after the sale, as well as installation of the product and training in its use.

In an interview with the sales team, you have discovered the following information:

1. The six salespeople on the team have a wide range of sales experience and knowledge of the products and services being offered. Two of them have been involved in the product's development but know little about sales. Two of them have excellent track records in selling software and technical products but know little about the new products and services. Another has some experience with the products and services and some sales experience. The last member is the brother-in-law of your company's CEO and has had some experience in real estate sales.

2. The former manager tried cross-training by sending them out on sales calls with salespeople who had different backgrounds. He also went on sales calls with each person to observe and provide feedback. He was not happy with the results

and felt that he was running out of time. The company had not made another sale in addition to the one made by the CEO.

3. The CEO indicates that you must have one sale per salesperson in three months or he will end the project. He has legitimate concern that the salespeople will be discouraged if they do not achieve this goal, and that they will have taken too much in pay advances against future sales to want to stay. The team knows that they each have three months within which to make one sale; this would allow the company to break even on the investment and provide each person with a living wage. Your salespeople receive a base salary and work on commission. To earn a living wage while they learn to sell the product, they have been taking pay advances that must be paid back with commissions.

4. The software product is very expensive—just over $100,000 for the product, installation, and training. Additionally, the customer pays $5,000 a month for customer-service support and guidance. The one company that purchased the product has had the software in place for only two months. From all indications, that company's increased profits would pay for the initial investment in six months and would then start producing a substantial profit.

5. There is no tracking system in place to manage the leads obtained from three sources: (1) referrals made by present customers, which are large financial institutions; (2) trade shows where salespeople meet potential customers; and (3) government reports that identify and qualify potential customers. The salespeople follow up on the leads.

6. The selling process is not defined, since there hasn't been a successful sale yet; the single sale was unique.

7. The best leads are generated by the large financial institutions, which invite mid-sized companies that are customers to attend a sales presentation. But only one of the decision makers needed to make the sale typically attends. The salespeople need to reach three decision makers—the CEO/owner, CFO, and IT manager—for the sale to be approved. These individuals need different information before they can contribute to the overall purchase decision.

8. Your salespeople indicate that they are becoming concerned about making the sales goal. They are well equipped with laptop computers and demo programs but lack a structured selling process and analysis of their progress. They have received feedback from each other and from the former sales manager when he went on sales calls with them. While they believe in the product and enjoy the job, they are becoming discouraged.

9. The sales team is a mixed group. While together they have what it takes to be successful, individually each one is lacking some knowledge and skills. Guidance from the former manager was limited at best, and feedback from their prospects has been nonexistent. All want to do a good job and appear to be highly motivated, but they do not know what it takes to become successful.

10. Because of time constraints, you have to move quickly to assess the situation, develop a solution, and put it in place.

The Performance Analysis

Use the Performance Analysis Worksheet (Figure 8-1) to do the following:

1. Describe the team's present level of performance, using both descriptive terms and measurable results.
2. Describe the long-term desired performance level, using both descriptive terms and measurable results.
3. Describe the reasonable goal, using both descriptive terms and measurable results.
4. Identify the factors working for and against closing the performance gap. Weight the impact of each factor on a scale of 1 to 4 and indicate its force by the length of the arrow.
5. Compare your results with the completed case study Performance Analysis Worksheet (Figure 8-2).

   The following comments explain how the Performance Analysis Worksheet factors were placed and weighted.

(text continued on p. 125)

FIGURE 8-1. BLANK PERFORMANCE ANALYSIS WORKSHEET

Present Level of Performance: ____________________

Desired Level of Performance: ____________________

Reasonable Goal: ____________________

Factors	Driving Forces					Restraining Forces			
	+4	+3	+2	+1	0	−1	−2	−3	−4
Information									
clear expectations	.	.	.	.		.	.	.	.
relevant feedback	.	.	.	.		.	.	.	.
relevant guides	.	.	.	.		.	.	.	.
performance coaching	.	.	.	.		.	.	.	.
Resources									
materials/tools	.	.	.	.		.	.	.	.
time	.	.	.	.		.	.	.	.
clear processes/procedures	.	.	.	.		.	.	.	.
safe/organized environment	.	.	.	.		.	.	.	.
Incentives									
financial incentives	.	.	.	.		.	.	.	.
other incentives	.	.	.	.		.	.	.	.
enriched jobs	.	.	.	.		.	.	.	.
positive work environment	.	.	.	.		.	.	.	.
Motives									
motives aligned with work	.	.	.	.		.	.	.	.
employees desire to perform	.	.	.	.		.	.	.	.
expectations are realistic	.	.	.	.		.	.	.	.
recruit/select the right people	.	.	.	.		.	.	.	.

(continues)

FIGURE 8-1. CONTINUED

Factors	Driving Forces					Restraining Forces			
	+4	+3	+2	+1	0	−1	−2	−3	−4
Capacity									
capacity to learn	.	.	.	.		.	.	.	.
capacity to do what is needed	.	.	.	.		.	.	.	.
recruit/select the right people	.	.	.	.		.	.	.	.
emotional limitations	.	.	.	.		.	.	.	.
Knowledge/Skills									
required knowledge	.	.	.	.		.	.	.	.
required skills	.	.	.	.		.	.	.	.
placement	.	.	.	.		.	.	.	.
cross-trained	.	.	.	.		.	.	.	.

FIGURE 8-2. COMPLETED PERFORMANCE ANALYSIS WORKSHEET FOR CASE STUDY

Present Level of Performance: A sales group of mixed readiness levels, with an inexperienced sales manager, in danger of floundering with no sales made to date.

Desired Level of Performance: A trained, confident, productive, and continuously improving sales team making three sales per salesperson per month within 18 months.

Reasonable Goal: A cross-trained sales team with one sale per salesperson within three months.

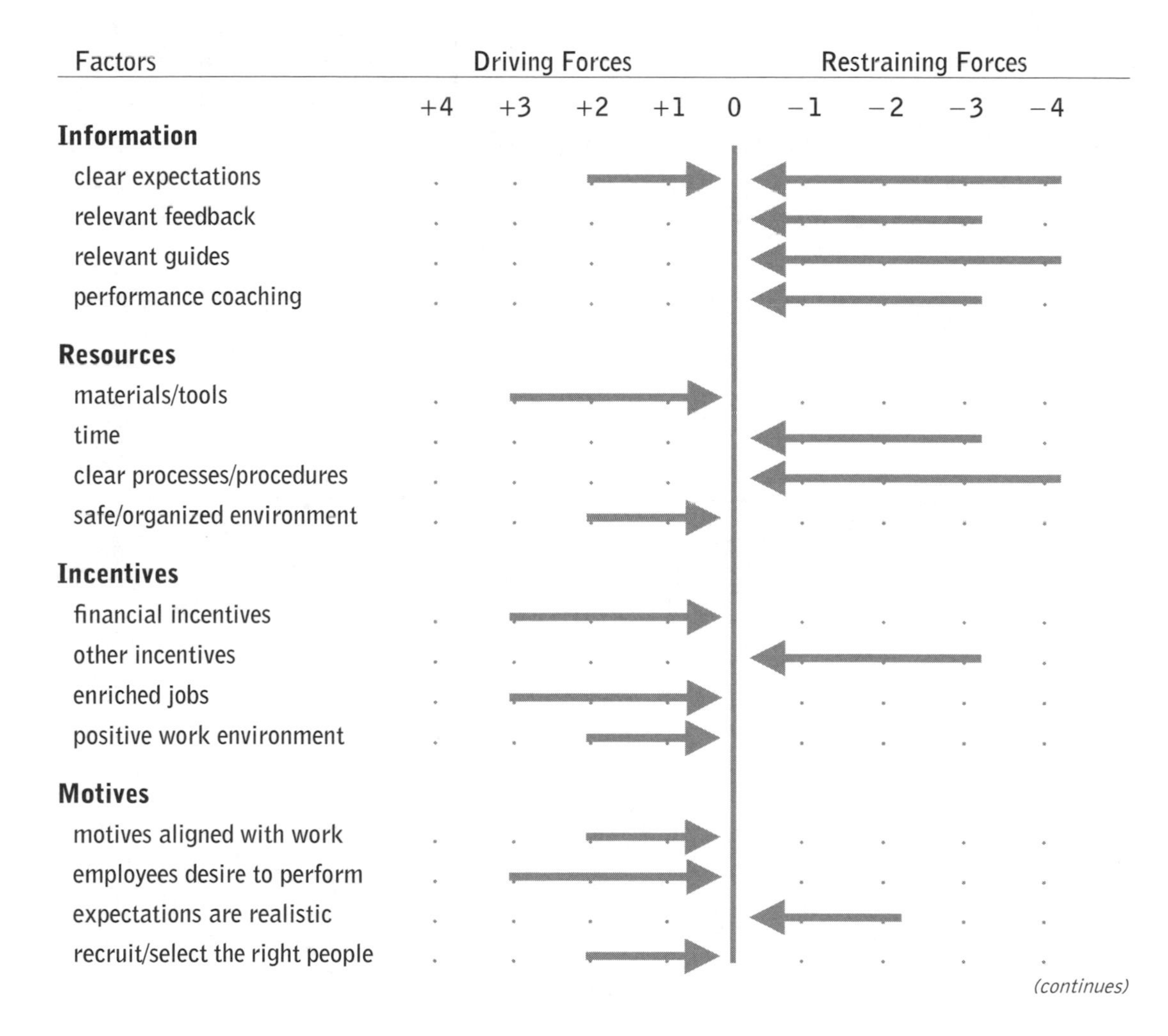

(continues)

FIGURE 8-2. CONTINUED

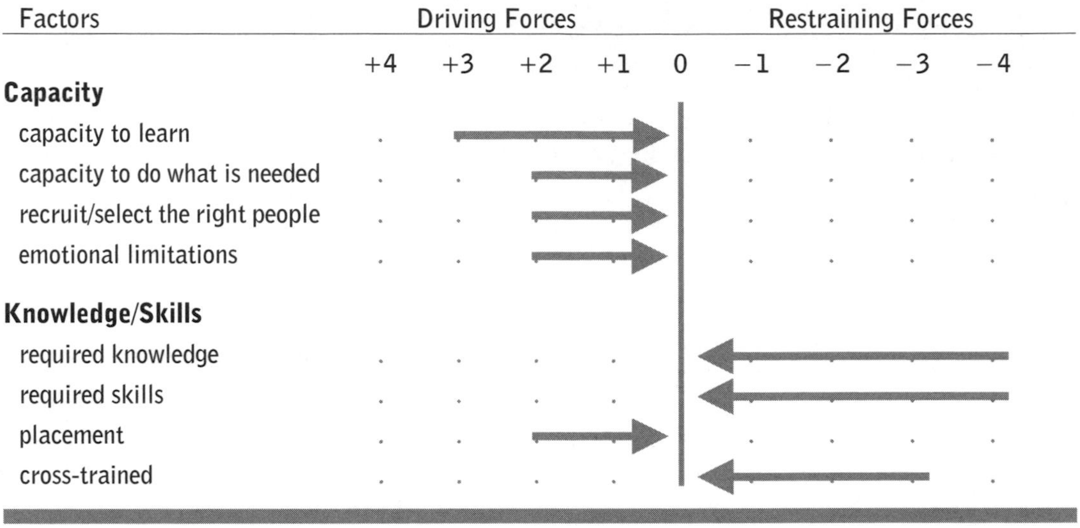

Factors	Driving Forces					Restraining Forces			
	+4	+3	+2	+1	0	−1	−2	−3	−4
Capacity									
capacity to learn									
capacity to do what is needed									
recruit/select the right people									
emotional limitations									
Knowledge/Skills									
required knowledge									
required skills									
placement									
cross-trained									

Factors	Driving Forces					Restraining Forces			
	+4	+3	+2	+1	0	−1	−2	−3	−4

Information

clear expectations

While there are clear expectations regarding the desired outcome (one sale per salesperson within three months), there are no clear expectations as to what activities are necessary to accomplish this.

relevant feedback

Feedback is very limited since the sales manager cannot routinely observe the salespeople in the selling process.

relevant guides

Since the selling process is not defined, there are no guidelines for the salespeople to follow.

performance coaching

Performance coaching can have very little effect without a clearly defined selling process.

Resources

materials/tools

The sales team has the necessary equipment to make sales calls.

time

The sales team is running out of time with only three months left.

clear processes/procedures

The selling process has not been clearly defined.

safe/organized environment

The work environment is safe and organized.

Incentives

financial incentives

The commission system provides financial incentives, although these can become a restraining force as the sales team draws more advances against future sales.

other incentives

There weren't any other incentives in place. With a low-readiness team like this one, there should have been incentives for doing the right activities since results are not immediate.

enriched jobs

The jobs are enriched in that they require a variety of skills, offer autonomy and responsibility, and allow the salesperson to identify with the selling process and the significance of the parts.

positive work environment

The overall work environment is positive.

Motives

motives aligned with work

The salespeople are there for the right reasons.

Factors | Driving Forces | Restraining Forces

+4 +3 +2 +1 0 −1 −2 −3 −4

employees desire to perform

All would like to succeed.

expectations are realistic

With no clear course of action, there are unclear expectations at all levels.

recruit/select the right people

With the exception of the CEO's brother-in-law, they all appear to have been selected well.

Capacity

capacity to learn

They all have the capacity to learn.

capacity to do what is needed

With proper direction and a clearly defined process, they should be able to do the job.

recruit/select the right people

The right people are in place.

emotional limitations

There are no obvious emotional limitations.

Knowledge/Skills

required knowledge

While they all have part of what is needed, no one is complete as a salesperson.

required skills

While they all have part of what is needed, no one is complete as a salesperson.

placement

No problem with placement.

cross-trained

Together as a team, they have the necessary knowledge and skills but need to be cross-trained to be effective as individuals.

Cause-Analysis Questions[2]

To assist you in analyzing a performance gap for your own workgroup, the following questions are provided. Please note that your meeting should begin with a discussion of present and desired levels of performance and should allow for employee participation in setting the reasonable goal for interim achievement.

These questions can also help you identify the impact of driving and restraining forces that you uncover when completing the Performance Analysis Worksheet. Each section starts with an open-ended question intended to promote discussion; follow-up direct questions should be used only if the matters have not been covered in the discussion.

A. Information

Open-ended, exploratory question: **Do you have the information you need to be successful in closing the performance gap?**

Direct, follow-up questions:

1. Do you know what needs to be done?
2. Are you receiving enough feedback from me regarding your performance?
3. Do you have clear and relevant performance aids to guide your work?
4. Am I providing the necessary direction and support you need to be successful?

B. Resources

Open-ended, exploratory question: **What additional materials, equipment, or other resources do you need to be successful?**

Direct, follow-up questions:

1. Do you have the materials and tools needed to do your job?
2. Do you have the time needed to do your job?
3. Do we have the necessary processes and procedures defined for you to be able to do your job?
4. Is the work environment safe, clean, organized, and conducive to excellent performance?

C. Incentives

Open-ended, exploratory question: **What else would you like to see implemented to encourage outstanding performance in the workplace?**

Direct, follow-up questions:

1. Are there sufficient financial incentives present to encourage excellent performance?
2. Are there other ways that we can encourage excellent performance?
3. Do you enjoy your job?
4. Is this a positive work environment where you feel you have the opportunity to succeed?

D. Motives

Open-ended, exploratory question: **What do you think of the incentives we have in place to encourage exceptional performance?**

Direct, follow-up questions:

1. Do you feel that this is a good place to work?
2. Do you desire to do your job to the best of your abilities?
3. Do you view the work environment as positive?
4. Are we the right people to do the job successfully?

E. Capacity

Open-ended, exploratory question: **Are you able to learn and do what is needed to be successful?**

Direct, follow-up questions:

1. Are you able to learn what is needed to get the job done?
2. Are you physically able to do your job?
3. Is there anything that is holding you back from doing your best?
4. Do we need people with different skills to do the job better?

F. Knowledge and Skills

Open-ended, exploratory question: **What additional training and skills do you need to be successful?**

Direct, follow-up questions:

1. Do you have the knowledge necessary to be successful at your job?
2. Do you have the skills needed to be successful at your job?
3. Is there a good match between your skills and the job?
4. Are there other jobs that you'd like to learn?

APPLICATION EXERCISE

Select a representative group of your employees to meet and discuss the performance gap that you identified in Chapter 7. Make sure you include some of the informal leaders in this group. Even though you have analyzed the gap on your own, start over again with your employees by describing the present and desired levels of performance, then ask for comments. Have them set a reasonable goal that will begin to close the gap over the next three to six months.

Show them the Performance Analysis Worksheet, and ask them to identify and weight the driving and restraining forces. Note: While the worksheet gives you structure, the cause-analysis questions will help you to lead the discussion.

Notes

1. This case study originally appeared in Roger Chevalier, "Updating the Behavioral Engineering Model," *Performance Improvement* 42, no. 5 (May/June 2003): 8–13.
2. The cause-analysis questions were first published in Roger Chevalier, "Leadership in Performance Consulting," *Handbook of Human Performance Technology*, 3rd ed. (San Francisco: Pfeiffer, 2006).

> "And a decision without an alternative is a desperate gambler's throw . . . ."
>
> —PETER DRUCKER

CHAPTER 9

Selecting the Best Solutions

With the Performance Analysis Worksheet as a starting point, you are ready to develop solutions to any performance gap. You do this by strengthening or adding the driving forces, weakening or removing the restraining forces, or, ideally, both. And since there are often a variety of causes for a performance gap, you may need to use a number of solutions to improve performance. In most cases, you will add new supports to improve performance while removing barriers to performance.

Solutions need to be selected on the basis of the causes of the problem, the costs involved, and the organization's culture. Primarily, you must make sure that the costs of the solutions you select are not greater than the benefits that will be derived. Likewise, if your solutions are not aligned with organizational culture, the odds of successful implementation are small.

Generating Potential Solutions

Each of the six areas of the cause-analysis model (information, resources, incentives, motives, capacity, and knowledge and skills) has potential solutions. Figure 9-1, derived from Figure 7-1 presented earlier, depicts the potentials in each area.

FIGURE 9-1. POTENTIAL SOLUTIONS FOR DIFFERENT CAUSES

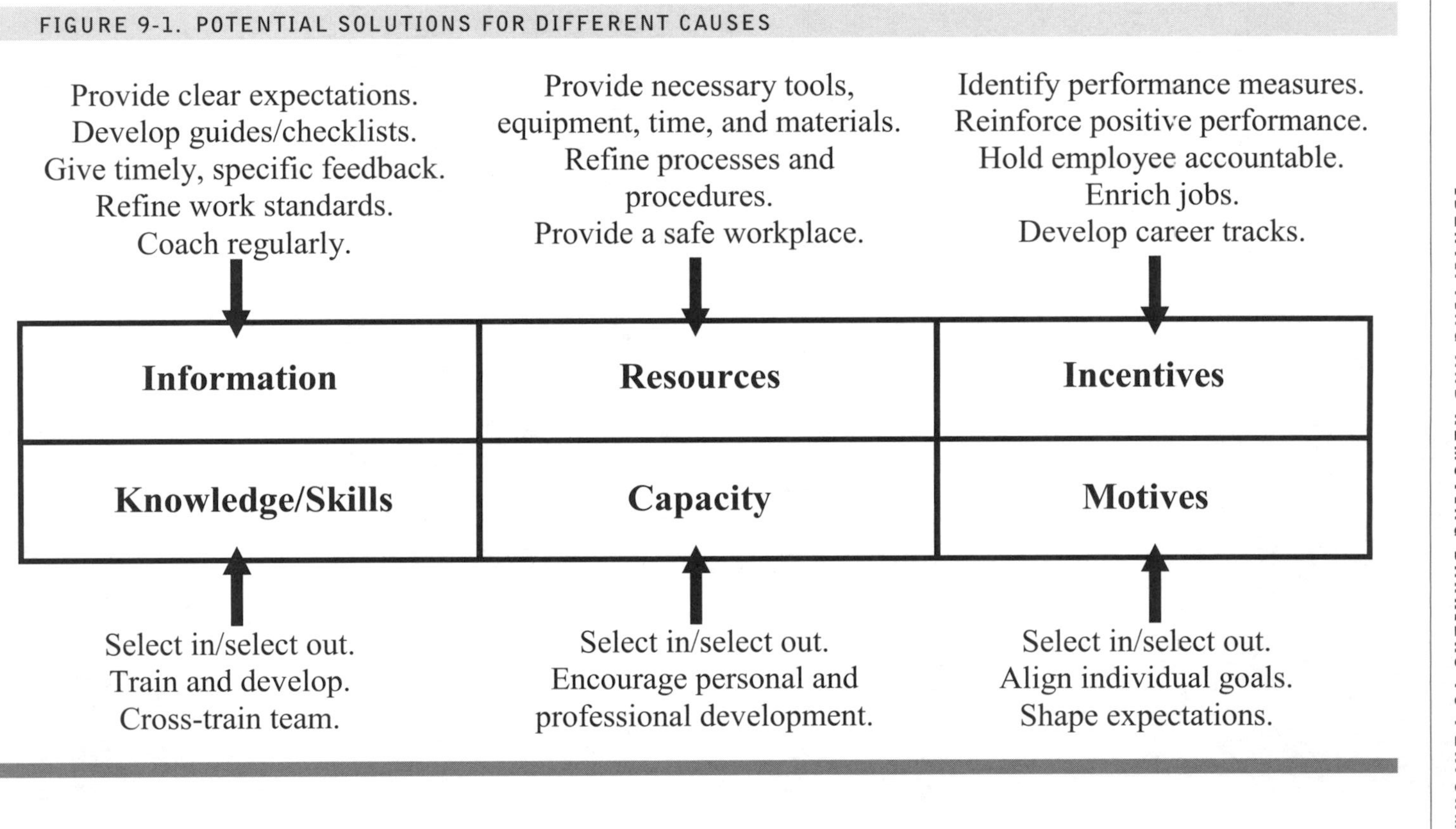

An important aspect of performance analysis is leveraging your solutions. That is, you want to leverage incentives, resources, and information solutions to support changes in knowledge, capacity, and motives. For example, changes in the work environment are more effective, and often a lot cheaper to make, than trying to change individuals. Stated another way, attempts to change the individuals you have on your team, through better selection and additional training, might not improve performance if you do not also change the environment to ensure that expectations are clearly stated, that adequate feedback and coaching are provided, that the necessary materials, time, and equipment are available, and that there are proper measurements and rewards for performance. Figure 9-2 depicts this leverage of individual-based solutions with changes in the work environment.[1]

FIGURE 9-2. LEVERAGING MULTIPLE PERFORMANCE SOLUTIONS

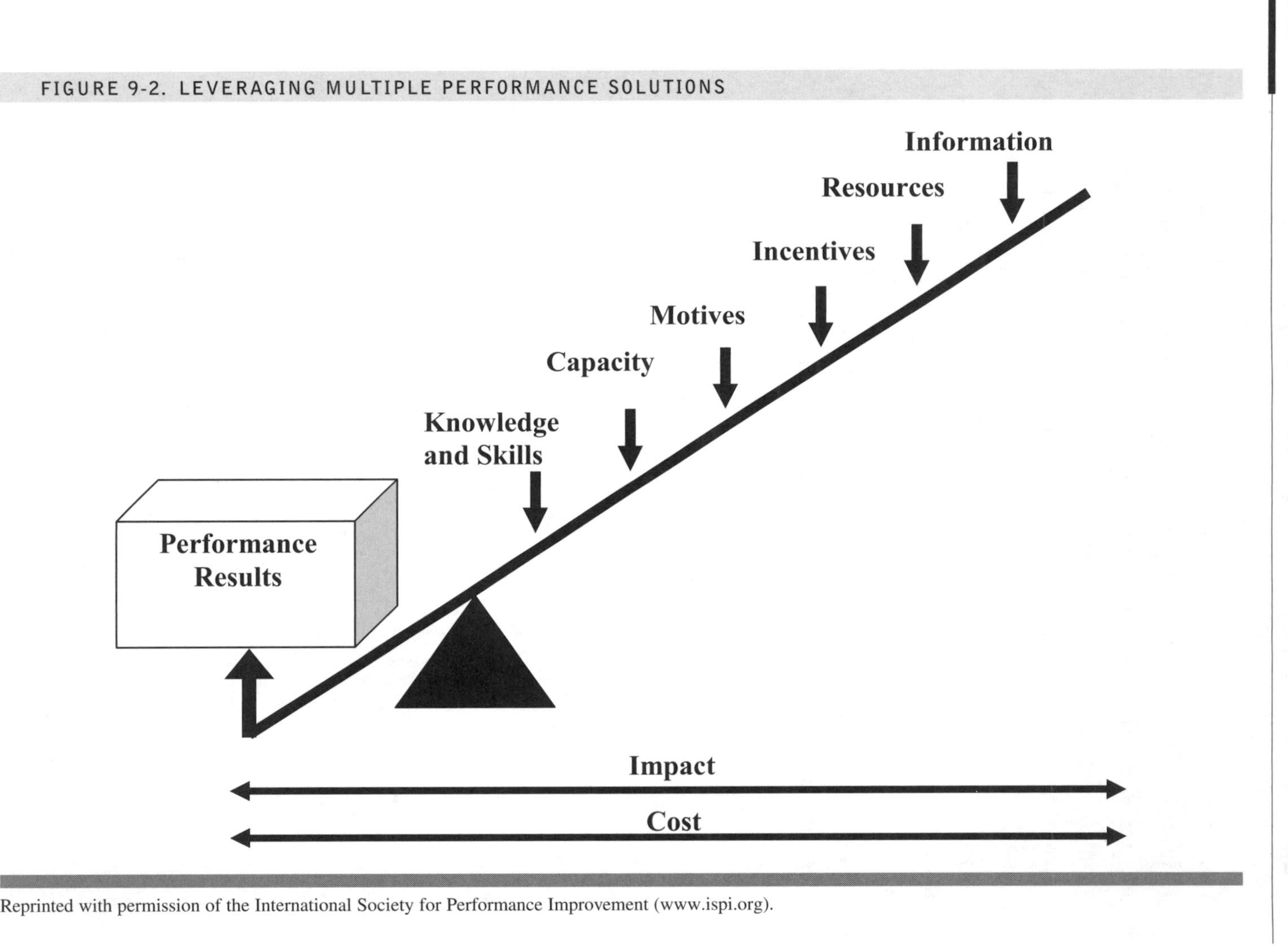

Developing Solutions for the Case Study

The following solutions were applied in the organization described in the case study given in Chapter 8.

Factors	Driving Forces					Restraining Forces			
	+4	+3	+2	+1	0	−1	−2	−3	−4

Information

clear expectations

Analysis: While there are clear expectations regarding the desired outcome (one sale per salesperson within three months), there are no clear expectations as to what activities are necessary to accomplish this. *Solution:* A clearly defined process with step-by-step procedures was developed and communicated to the sales team.

relevant feedback

Analysis: Feedback is very limited since the sales manager cannot routinely observe the salespeople in the selling process. *Solution:* A customer feedback system was developed that provided each salesperson with an evaluation of his or her performance on a postcard sent directly by the customer after each sales call. The salesperson received a copy of the card immediately while the sales manager's assistant developed profiles of each salesperson's strengths and weaknesses as perceived by their customers.

relevant guides

Analysis: Since the selling process is not defined, there are no guides for the salespeople to follow. *Solution:* Once the selling process was defined, checklists and other guides were developed to assist the salespeople in following the process.

performance coaching

Analysis: Performance coaching can have very little effect without a clearly defined selling process. *Solution:* Armed with the customer feedback and a clearly defined selling process, the sales manager was able to give timely, specific feedback to each salesperson.

Resources

materials/tools

Analysis: The sales team has the necessary equipment to make sales calls. *Solution:* No change for this factor was necessary or implemented.

time

Analysis: The sales team is running out of time with only three months left. *Solution:* The element of time was discussed with the sales team and re-framed to be a driving force for changing the way they were selling immediately.

clear processes/procedures

Analysis: The selling process has not been clearly defined. *Solution:* The selling process was clearly defined and integrated into the expectations given to the salespeople, provided on the customer feedback form, and a part of the sales manager's feedback.

Factors	Driving Forces					Restraining Forces			
	+4	+3	+2	+1	0	−1	−2	−3	−4

safe/organized environment

Analysis: The work environment is safe and organized. *Solution:* No change for this factor was necessary or implemented.

Incentives

financial incentives

Analysis: The commission system provides financial incentives although these can become a restraining force as the sales team draws more advances against future sales. *Solution:* To avoid this becoming a restraining force, past draws against future commissions were cancelled so that the salespeople could see themselves as earning a living wage if they were successful from that point forward.

other incentives

Analysis: There weren't any other incentives in place. With a low-readiness team like this one, there should have been incentives for doing the right activities since results are not immediate. *Solution:* Many nonfinancial incentives were developed to encourage the appropriate activities necessary to be successful. Incentives were mostly psychological in nature, but some inexpensive gifts were also used as rewards.

enriched jobs

Analysis: The jobs are enriched in that they require a variety of skills, offer autonomy and responsibility, and allow the salesperson to identify with the selling process. *Solution:* No change for this factor was necessary or implemented.

positive work environment

Analysis: The overall work environment is positive. *Solution:* No change for this factor was necessary or implemented.

Motives

motives aligned with work

Analysis: The salespeople are there for the right reasons. *Solution:* By clearly defining expectations and providing specific feedback, this factor was strengthened.

employees desire to perform

Analysis: All would like to succeed. *Solution:* By clearly defining expectations and providing specific feedback, this factor was also strengthened.

expectations are realistic

Analysis: With no clear course of action, there are unclear expectations at all levels. *Solution:* By clearly defining expectations and providing specific feedback, the negative impact of this factor was weakened.

recruit/select the right people

Analysis: With the exception of the CEO's brother-in-law, the salespeople all appear to have been selected well. *Solution:* The CEO's brother-in-law was eventually fired for his poor performance and for being a liability to the team.

Factors	Driving Forces					Restraining Forces			
	+4	+3	+2	+1	0	−1	−2	−3	−4

Capacity

capacity to learn

Analysis: They all have the capacity to learn. *Solution:* The only salesperson with a problem in this area was fired.

capacity to do what is needed

Analysis: With proper direction and a clearly defined process, they should be able to do the job. *Solution:* The only salesperson with a problem in this area was fired.

recruit/select the right people

Analysis: The right people are in place. *Solution:* There was not enough time to recruit, select, and train new people, so this factor was not changed except for the firing of the CEO's brother-in-law.

emotional limitations

Analysis: There are no obvious emotional limitations. *Solution:* No change for this factor was necessary or implemented.

Knowledge/Skills

required knowledge

Analysis: While they all have part of what is needed, no one is complete as a salesperson. *Solution:* A training program was used to define the selling process and to communicate expectations clearly.

required skills

Analysis: While they all have part of what is needed, no one is complete as a salesperson. *Solution:* The salespeople were cross-trained to learn from each other's strengths.

placement

Analysis: No problem with placement. *Solution:* No change for this factor was necessary or implemented.

cross-trained

Analysis: Together as a team, they have the necessary knowledge and skills but need to be cross-trained to be effective as individuals. *Solution:* The salespeople were cross-trained to learn from each other's strengths.

What Happened in the Real Case

In the case study, the new sales manager was looking to training to enhance the skills of his team, but he also knew a broader solution was needed: to build the systems that would systematically track leads and sales, as well as provide feedback that would continuously improve the performance of his people. Additionally, he would need a way to bridge the gap between sales and customer service.

Immediate Solutions

Sixteen hours of sales and customer service training were delivered in a weekend workshop. The consultant provided the structure by presenting various sales and customer service models, and he cross-trained the participants as they moved from the generic models to practical courses of action. During this training, a clear selling process was developed as well.

For instance, two sales-management systems were developed from the coaching and sales performance aids and from the employee input received during the training programs. The systems focused on the *means* (how salespeople were perceived by their clients) as well as the *ends* (how clients moved through the "sales funnel" to become customers).

A client and customer survey, derived from the sales performance guide, was developed to be used in gathering information from clients and customers regarding the selling process and the value of the products and services being offered. First, a short postcard survey was set up to gain customer feedback on all sales calls. Second, as soon as a lead would be declared dead, a one-page survey would be sent to the failed prospect. Third, a more comprehensive two-page survey would be sent to customers after the purchase was made, the software installed, and the first month of service provided. When the surveys were returned, a copy would be immediately given to the salesperson. The sales manager's administrative assistant would analyze the feedback on each salesperson and prepare a monthly summary for the sales manager, who would then provide feedback on selling tendencies and ways for each salesperson to become more effective.

A parallel survey was also developed to gather information every three months from the salespeople regarding the leadership they were receiving from the sales manager. The net effect would be to develop an interrelated survey system for the regular assessment and continuous improvement of the sales and coaching processes. Ongoing customer service surveys would later be developed to bring that division under the same system.

Long-Term Results and Conclusions

While training was the initial part of this intervention, use of performance evaluation provided systematic assessment and continuous improvement for the new sales team. Tracking individual and collective performance after the training encouraged employee use of what was learned in the classroom while providing an ongoing source of feedback with which to improve performance.

As mentioned at the beginning, sales managers have a difficult leadership task in that they do not routinely observe much of the work done by their salespeople. The client and customer surveys developed in this case empowered sales managers with the information necessary to coach their teams to improve performance. The client, customer, and salesperson feedback received via the various surveys also served to identify specific knowledge and skill deficiencies in the sales team. These were remedied with short training sessions held during the weekly sales meeting and were presented by either the sales manager, one of the salespeople, or the outside consultant. The weekly sales meeting also served to reinforce the idea that the salespeople were members of a team rather than individuals working on their own. Salespeople who were on the road phoned in to participate in the one-hour meetings whenever possible. The agenda allowed salespeople to describe their progress and get credit for their victories by ringing a bell for each victory.

The weekly sales meeting was designed to improve team performance by shaping group norms. While the emphasis was on assessing progress and reinforcing success, the final part of the agenda allowed each member of the sales team to talk about what was happening in their personal lives to further build esprit de corps. This team-building process was complemented by having salespeople attend various marketing programs to work together and with clients.

The combination of these interventions provided the needed training and built a basic sales system that helped the fledgling sales team surpass all sales goals during the first two quarters following the training while developing a strong foundation for their future success. Bringing the customer service team under the same systematic assessment and continuous improvement survey system the following quarter further integrated the two divisions. The group made its sales goal of one sale per salesperson within in the third month by making five sales and by terminating one salesperson. They went on to great success and were eventually acquired by a major software producer.

Tips on Selecting the Best Solutions

Follow these suggestions for picking the solutions to performance problems that will ultimately yield the best results.

- Once the causes of a performance gap are determined, you are ready to select the appropriate solutions needed to improve workplace performance.
- Since there are usually multiple causes for a performance gap, you will need to use multiple solutions to close that gap.
- Solutions should take into account the causes of the problem, the costs of making a change, and the culture of your organization.
- Changes at the individual level should be leveraged with changes in the work environment.

APPLICATION EXERCISE

Revisit the Performance Analysis Worksheet that you developed with your staff. Identify the driving forces that you will strengthen or add as well as the restraining forces that you will weaken or remove. Now select the solutions you will use to improve performance, taking into account the causes of the performance gap, the cost of each solution, and the culture of your organization. To have the greatest impact, remember to leverage changes at the individual level with changes at the work environment level.

Note

1. International Society for Performance Improvement Online Institute, *Principles and Practices of Human Performance Technology Participant Manual* (Silver Spring, MD: ISPI, 2001).

"It's not the strongest of the species who survive, not the most intelligent, but the ones most responsive to change."

—CHARLES DARWIN

CHAPTER 10

Managing Change

One of the most important roles that you have as a manager is that of managing change. This chapter provides the guidance you need to plan for and implement changes to improve workplace performance.

A Manager's Ability to Cause Change[1]

Many managers believe that if they change the knowledge of an individual or group, that a behavior change will invariably follow. Unfortunately, this is not always the case. As stated earlier in this book, about 85 percent of performance issues are the result of environmental factors and are not the individual's fault. You should therefore focus more energy on improving the work environment and stop trying to fix the individuals who work for you.

Training and other forms of participative change should be part of a more comprehensive performance-improvement strategy. By focusing on the work environment, you will develop a change strategy that complements the training you also provide.

The Power to Change

The starting point for any discussion of change strategies is an understanding of what power is and how it is used to implement change. A very useful way to understand a manager's power is to divide it into two distinct areas: personal power and position power.[2]

Personal power is the strength that comes when you gain the confidence and trust of others (based on their perception of your personality, competence, and integrity) and it is the basis for participative change. *Position power* is the authority to reward or sanction your employees, and it is the basis for directive change.

In training, a *participative change* begins as the instructor uses personal power to deliver new ideas to an individual or group, with the belief that if their knowledge and attitudes can be changed, then a change in behavior will invariably follow. This strategy is effective only with employees who are ready to change and will return to an environment that supports the change. This is a bottom-up approach in which a manager uses involvement to gain the commitment of those who must change.

Position power can be used to implement a *directive change* more quickly by communicating expectations and shaping behavior with new systems and work processes. The problem is that a directive change may be resisted. While a manager can quickly impact group and individual behavior with position power, the change may have little impact on attitudes. In other words, mandated change may lead to short-term compliance but not to long-term commitment. This is a top-down approach that holds people accountable as the means of ensuring compliance by those who must change.

Preparation, Change, and Reinforcement

Many change strategies fail because the individual or group is not prepared to change, or the changed behavior is not reinforced. Managers should use a total change strategy of preparation, implementation, and reinforcement. These phases of change are some times referred to as *unfreezing*, *changing*, and *refreezing*.[3]

Preparing for the Change (Unfreezing)

Unfreezing is not always necessary, as sometimes the individual or group has realized that the present way of working is no longer getting the results wanted. But sometimes, the individual or group is unaware of, or does not care that the results do not meet, the standard that has been set. If your employees are not prepared to change, and you can't wait for them to discover the need to change, you will have to unfreeze them, thus preparing them for change.

There are many ways to prepare or make your workgroup ready for change. The most common way is to explain the situation and solicit input. Another way is to allow an individual or group to fail and thus become dissatisfied with the present way. Of course, this should be done in such a way that does not risk injury or impose a negative financial impact. In essence, you are trying to get the individual or group to let go of a way of working that is not producing the desired results.

For example, when I was teaching one of my sons to drive, I worked with him as he learned to drive with a standard transmission. He became fairly proficient in driving around our town, which has no hills. The day he received word that he had passed his driving test, and was now licensed, he announced that he was going to take a trip to San Francisco, about 35 miles south of where we live.

I could foresee problems with his driving a stick shift in San Francisco, with its very steep hills. I could have tried to tell him about the problem, but I don't think he would have listened. Instead, I asked if we could take one more ride together. I had him drive to the hilly farmland that surrounds our town. I had him stop on a steep hill where there was no traffic and asked him to pretend that he was on a hill in San Francisco, stopped at a red light. To complete the scene, I told him that an imaginary car had just pulled up three feet behind him, and the light had just turned green. As he tried to shift his feet from the brake to the clutch, the car rolled backward. I started yelling at him as if I were in the imaginary car behind him: "You hit my new car! Who taught you how to drive, you dumb ^*$#*@!" My son now realized that he wasn't ready to drive in San Francisco and was willing to practice using the parking brake until he learned how to "ride the clutch" to deal with being stopped on a hill. He had over a month of practicing in the local hills before he made the trip to San Francisco.

Unfreezing is a systematic way of breaking down someone's habits of doing things the old way so that he or she accepts a new alternative. The present way of doing business must be challenged so that the need for change is accepted.

Learning the New Way (Changing)

Once the individual or workgroup realizes that the old ways of doing business no longer work, or when you have helped them see that they will no longer be successful, they are ready to change. There are three strategies for change: compliance, identification, and internalization.

1. *Compliance* is accomplished by using your position power and telling the individual or workgroup that change is necessary. If the individual or group perceives that you have enough position power, there will be compliance with, but not necessarily commitment to, the change. Compliance can be a way of unfreezing a group, or it can be a way of bypassing the preparation stage. But in either case, though the change will happen quickly, it may not be permanent.

2. *Identification* encourages change based on trust and is effected through personal power. It works only with an individual or workgroup that is prepared to change and is willing to follow the example of an instructor or other role model. Identification requires that individuals be prepared to change; it takes longer to affect performance than does compliance, but it produces a more permanent form of change.

3. *Internalization* is not a way to bring about change, so much as it is the desired process. The individual or workgroup learns the new behavior and adopts it. In effect, the changes have been internalized, making the new behaviors the natural and correct ones. The starting point for internalization can be either compliance or identification, followed by acceptance and acknowledgment by the individual or group of the value of the change.

Reinforcing the Change (Refreezing)

When an individual or workgroup experiences a change in work habits or procedures, there's usually some anxiety about doing things differently. You must set reasonable goals for the individual or group to make the change and provide positive reinforcement as the change affects behavior. Regular reinforcement is necessary if the behavior is to be continued.

Change Process Case Study: Officer Candidate School

I lived through the change process in my personal life at Coast Guard Officer Candidate School (OCS). The unfreezing began the moment I arrived, as my civilian clothes were taken from me and were replaced with a uniform. My hair was cut short to make me look like everyone else. My contacts with the outside world were restricted to one telephone call each week. My life was given a new structure as I was forced to comply with the orders I was given. My only alternative was to quit and end up as an enlisted man in the Coast Guard, and that didn't sound like a good alternative to me.

Demerits were given for noncompliance, but they were removed for each week in which no demerits were received. I had real problems with change, and so I received 75 demerits in the first five weeks of training. I knew that I would be thrown out if I reached 100 in the seventeen weeks it took to complete the program. Because of all the demerits, I was sent to our platoon adviser, a senior officer who had no connection to the training process. He allowed me to relax in his office and asked me about my past. I told him I was married and had worked my way through college. He then said that he thought he knew my problem: I was taking OCS too seriously. I needed to see it as a game and play it to win. Following his advice, I never got another demerit.

The Coast Guard had intended that my platoon officer be my role model, but instead they supplied me with another, the platoon adviser who gave me the means to survive. Thanks to him, I started on what turned out to be a marvelous career. His other words of advice were on a small sign that he had on his desk: "*Non illigentium carborundum est,*" which, loosely translated, means "Don't let the bastards get you down." This phrase saved me many times in my Coast Guard career and in my other jobs that have followed. It's funny the things that we decide to internalize.

Participative vs. Directive Change

Participative change, as mentioned earlier in the chapter, uses personal power based on the employee's perception of the manager's or trainer's personality, competence, and integrity. The goal for the manager is to gain commitment to a change by allowing employees to participate in the change process, so that employees feel involved and empowered. Participative change tends to be a slow process; change is gradual and evolves. It is a bottom-up approach that focuses on selling and guiding the employee.

Directive change, also mentioned earlier, is based on position power, or the manager's authority to reward and hold others accountable. Using position power to effect change will lead to compliance, not commitment, since it involves informing and controlling others. The results are immediate, in that you tell employees what to do and structure the work environment. Figure 10-1 shows the key elements of participative and directive change.

Many effective change strategies involve the use of both position and personal power. The directive strategy overcomes inertia and creates some movement toward

FIGURE 10-1. STRATEGIES FOR EFFECTING CHANGE

Participative Change	Directive Change
Personal power	Position power
Commitment	Compliance
Involve/empower	Inform/control
Gradual change	Immediate change
Evolutionary	Revolutionary
Bottom-up	Top-down
Sell/guide	Tell/structure

the desired change. The participative strategy then trains the target group by adding new knowledge to affect attitudes. Many times these change-agent roles are played by different people—someone who "turns up the heat" with position power and another who "puts out the fires" with personal power.

An example to show how participative and directive change strategies are used together is the effort that has been made to get people to use seatbelts in their cars. Despite extensive educational programs, seatbelt use was not the norm in many states until the laws were changed. A combination of education and sanctions was necessary to change the behavior of many drivers.

Similarly, a manager should use both participative-change strategies (such as training and group decision making) and directive-change strategies (such as changing work processes and management systems) for a comprehensive change strategy that improves performance. While its original source is unknown, Figure 10-2 shows how participative and directive change improve workplace performance.[4]

Participative change alters the knowledge of the individual or workgroup to substitute more preferable attitudes, which then leads to changed individual and organizational behavior. Directive change impacts organizational and individual behavior more quickly and then changes the knowledge underlying the change. For the latter, existing attitudes are the last thing to change, and may remain unaffected because the individual or group is merely complying with directions.

Examples of methods of participative change include training, coaching, modeling, shared decision making, focus groups, quality circles, and autonomous workgroups. Examples of directive change methods include modification of work processes, operating procedures, and performance management; measurement, evaluation, compensation, and reward systems; and restructuring, reorganizing, or changing resources. Figure 10-3 provides examples of participative and directive change.

Tips on Managing Change

Follow these tips when you contemplate making changes in individual or group behavior.

FIGURE 10-2. LEVELS OF CHANGE

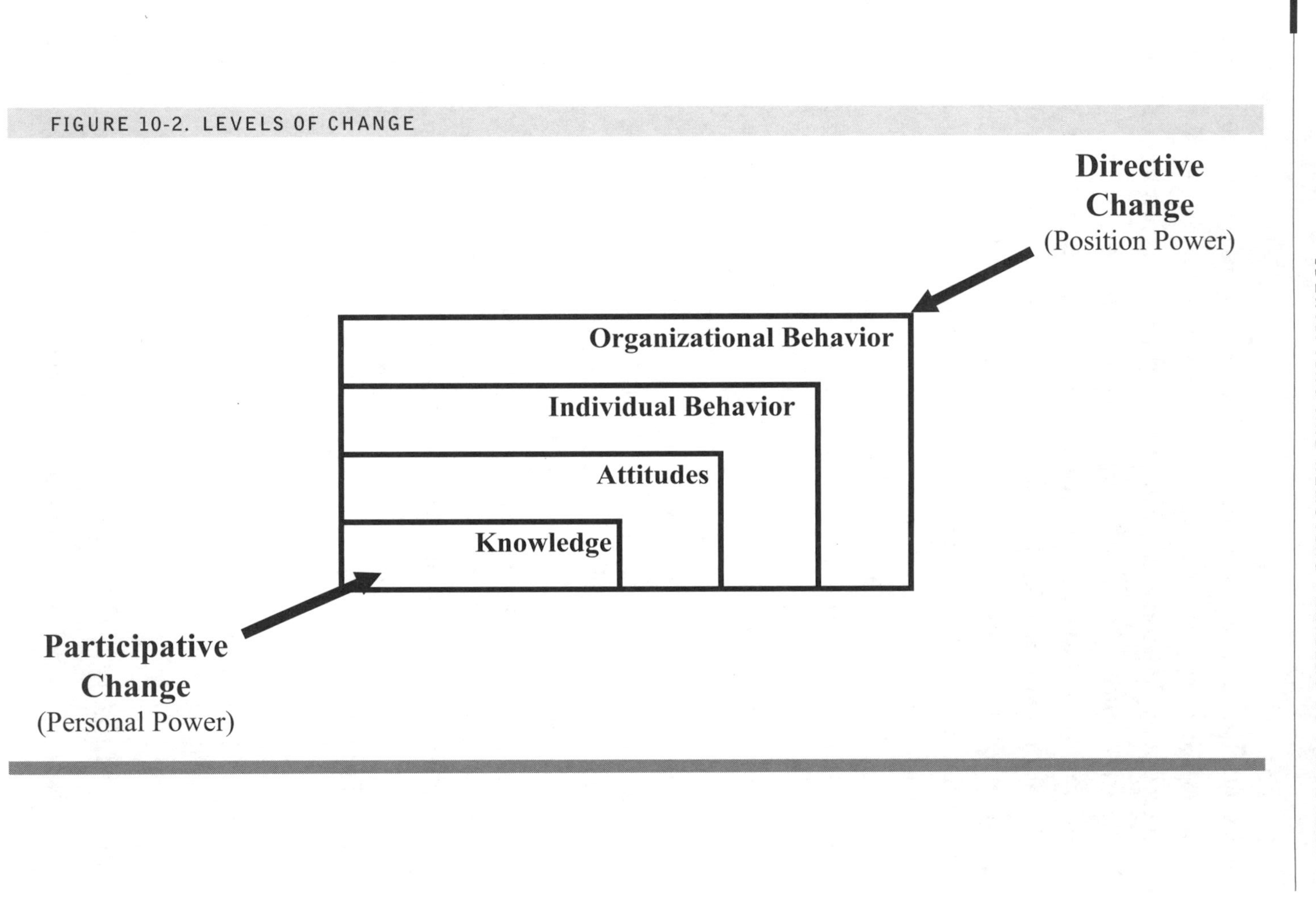

- Power is the basis for implementing change.
- Position power is the authority given to you to use in your formal role in your organization; it gives you the ability to offer rewards and hold employees accountable.
- Personal power is given to you by others based on their perception of your personality, competence, and integrity.
- The three phases of change are unfreezing, changing, and refreezing.
- Participative change is based on your use of personal power and gains commitment from your employees; examples of participative change include training, coaching, and shared decision making.
- Directive change is based on your use of position power and gets compliance from your employees; examples of directive change include changing work procedures, measurement systems, and reward systems.
- Most successful change strategies have elements of both directive and participative change.

FIGURE 10-3. EXAMPLES OF PARTICIPATIVE AND DIRECTIVE CHANGE

Participative Change	Directive Change
Training	Work processes
Coaching	Operating procedures
Modeling/identification	Performance management
Shared decision making	Measurement/evaluation
Focus groups	Compensation/rewards
Quality circles	Restructuring/reorganizing
Autonomous workgroups	Resource allocation

APPLICATION EXERCISE

You have determined the performance gap, identified the causes of the gap, set a reasonable goal, and determined what needs to be changed. You now need to decide how to prepare your workgroup for change and what types of changes are necessary. Using the Change Strategy Worksheet, Figure 10-4, describe how you will prepare your workgroup for change and what elements of participative and directive change you will use. (For a larger version of this and the other application exercise forms, visit www.aboutiwp.com.)

FIGURE 10-4. WORKSHEET FOR IMPLEMENTING CHANGE

Change Strategy Worksheet

Describe the readiness level of your workgroup for the change. ______

______

______

If the group's readiness level for the change is low, how will you prepare them for the change?

______

______

______

______

What elements of participative change will you use? ______

______

______

______

What elements of directive change will you use? ______

______

______

______

How will you reinforce your people after the change to ensure that they continue? ______

______

______

Notes

1. This material originally appeared in Roger Chevalier, "HPT: The Power to Change," *Performance Improvement* 29, no. 1 (2000): 23–25.
2. Amatai Etzioni, *A Comparative Analysis of Organizations* (New York: Holt, Rinehart, and Winston, 1961).
3. Kurt Lewin, "Frontiers in Group Dynamics: Concept, Method, and Reality in Social Science, Social Equilibria, and Social Change," *Human Relations* 1, no. 1 (June 1947): 5–41.
4. Paul Hersey and Kenneth H. Blanchard, "The Management of Change: Change and the Use of Power," *Training and Development Journal* 26, no. 1 (January 1972): 6–10.

"Count what is countable, measure what is measurable. What is not measurable, make measurable."

—GALILEO GALILEI

CHAPTER 11

Evaluating the Results of Performance-Improvement Initiatives

As a manager, you are responsible for the performance of your employees. Performance is the activity—what your people need to do to be successful—and the result is what is accomplished. You observe your employees to see that they are doing what is expected, and you measure the results to make sure that the outcome meets the goals for performance.

This chapter focuses on how to evaluate the results of the training your people receive and on how to evaluate the success of your attempts to improve performance.

Assessing the Value and Outcome of Training

One of the ways you may choose to improve the productivity of your employees is by putting them through some additional training—what is termed a *training intervention*. Training interventions can be divided into two groups: those that are controlled by others and those that are controlled by you. Classroom instruction, use of simulators, laboratory training, and computer-based training are usually provided by others; self-study is a type of training intervention controlled by individual employees, who might be trying to improve their knowledge and skills; and examples of training that you control are on-the-job training, mentoring, coaching, and team building.

A manager has control over most of nontraining interventions. For instance, you are responsible for the information given to your people, the documentation of their performance, the feedback offered, the job aids provided, the design of the work, the organizational structure, and the consequences for how the job is done and the results produced. You are also responsible for the individual and group behavior of your employees, in that you guide them through the processes and procedures they use to get the work done. You have at least partial control over the factors that influence behavior, such as leadership and coaching, the way performance is measured and rewarded, and the tools and equipment they have to do the work, as well as the selection and development of your workgroup. The culture of your organization is out of your control, yet that can also influence the way you and your employees do your jobs. Figure 11-1 is an outline of training and nontraining interventions, as well as the activities and results controlled by a manager.

What You Need to Know About Training

To get the most out of the training you offer your employees, you need to control what is taught in the courses to ensure that they receive the knowledge and skills necessary to be successful on the job. You also must ensure that the work environment reinforces what they have learned, so they use that newly acquired skill and knowledge on the job. Lastly, you need to provide feedback to the trainers so they can continue to be useful to you.

Training is a major investment. The training staff spends time and money analyzing what knowledge and skills the employees need, they design and develop the courses, and then they deliver those courses. There is a corresponding major investment in time, in that your people are away from the job while in the training.

FIGURE 11-1. INTERVENTIONS, ACTIVITIES, AND RESULTS

Training Interventions	Nontraining Interventions	Activities	Results/Value
• Classroom • Simulator • Laboratory • Computer-Based Training (CBT) • Self-study • On-the-job training* • Mentoring* • Coaching* • Team building*	• Information* • Documentation* • Feedback* • Job aids* • Workplace design* • Organizational structure* • Empowerment* • Measurement* • Consequences* (rewards/sanctions)	Individual Behaviors and Organizational Behaviors • Work practices • Work Processes Mitigating Factors • Leadership/coaching* • Measurement* • Incentives* • Tools/equipment* • Staffing* • Culture	• Quantity** • Quality** • Time** • Cost** • Productivity** • Sales** • Calls on warranty** • Customer retention** • Profitability** • Market share**
*Controlled by you	*Controlled by you	*Controlled by you	**Measured outputs

Since training is an expensive way to improve performance, you need to make sure there is a return on this investment. Managers have traditionally asked questions like:

- "Did you like the training?"
- "How many people attended the course?"
- "What did you learn?"

But with more of a bottom-line orientation, you should also be asking:

- "How are you using what you've learned?"
- "Are there other things you need to apply what you've learned?"
- "How has the training you received impacted your on-the-job performance?"
- "What is our return on investment for the training?"

Get the answers to these questions by evaluating the training your people receive. While the training staff systematically evaluates training in terms of its application on the job and its impact on organizational results, in most cases the results are measured by the employee's reaction to the training and a test of what has been learned.[1] Instead, you need to be sure that the training is applied to the work and that there is a positive and measurable impact on group performance.

The Evaluation of Training

The training staff routinely evaluates the training they provide during the design, development, and implementation stages to ensure quality and consistency. Generally they get input from experts or users to review what is being taught, or they use a pilot test of the course to provide feedback. Unfortunately, this is where the evaluation usually stops.

What needs to follow is an evaluation of the graduates to see whether they have applied what they learned. This can be done by direct observation, by surveys of the graduates and their supervisors, by measurement of performance indicators for the activities involved (such as quality, productivity, or customer satisfaction), and/or by measurement of a business outcome (such as number of sales, calls on warranty, customer retention, profitability, or market share).

There are four levels of evaluation to determine the impact of training.[2] Level 1 focuses on the reaction of individuals to the training or other performance-improvement interventions. These are commonly described as "smile sheets," as they report the reactions of students to the training. Alas, while end-of-course questionnaires provide immediate feedback, they are not good indicators of whether the students will apply what they have learned.[3]

Level 2 assesses what has been learned via end-of-course tests. All too often, these tests are knowledge-based, asking students questions about what they have learned. A better end-of-course test is performance-based, evaluating students' ability to perform the same tasks that are required on the job. While most Level 2 evaluations are limited to end-of-course tests, pre-tests are helpful in determining what students know before the training, and then the difference between the pre-test and the post-test indicates what was actually learned during the training.

Level 3 measures how much of what has been learned is actually applied to the workplace. By observing the graduate on the job or by surveying the graduates and their supervisors, you can determine how much training was transferred to the job. Your role is to ensure that the training is applied and that there is a sustained level of consistency for productivity (how much they produce), quality (how well they produce it), time it takes to do their job, and costs (such as waste).

Level 4 measures the impact of training on a designated business outcome, such as improved sales, decreased calls on warranty, increased customer retention and referrals, and higher profitability and market share. This is where the return on investment for training should occur. Despite making expensive investments in training, very few organizations determine whether that training actually improved organizational performance.[4]

Evaluation not only measures the impact of training but also encourages participants to use what was learned because it focuses attention on that training. By evaluating the impact of your training programs, you will also encourage the use of the knowledge and skills that were taught. As a manager, you are responsible for Level 3 evaluation to ensure that the training is applied and for Level 4 evaluation to ensure that the training improves individual and group performance.

Assessing Performance-Improvement Interventions

A manager evaluates the performance-improvement initiatives that he or she has imposed on the individual or workgroup. In the short term, you need to observe the activity or behavior of your people; this is a Level 3 evaluation that determines how *successful* you were in the short term. In the long term, you need to evaluate the impact of the intervention on your group and on the organization as a whole; this is a Level 4 evaluation that shows how *effective* you have been in the long term. Figure 11-2 portrays the two levels of evaluation.

Your initial focus after employees go through training, or after an intervention that you make, is to determine whether the employees are doing the job the way it should be done. Note that it is not sufficient to determine the effectiveness of the

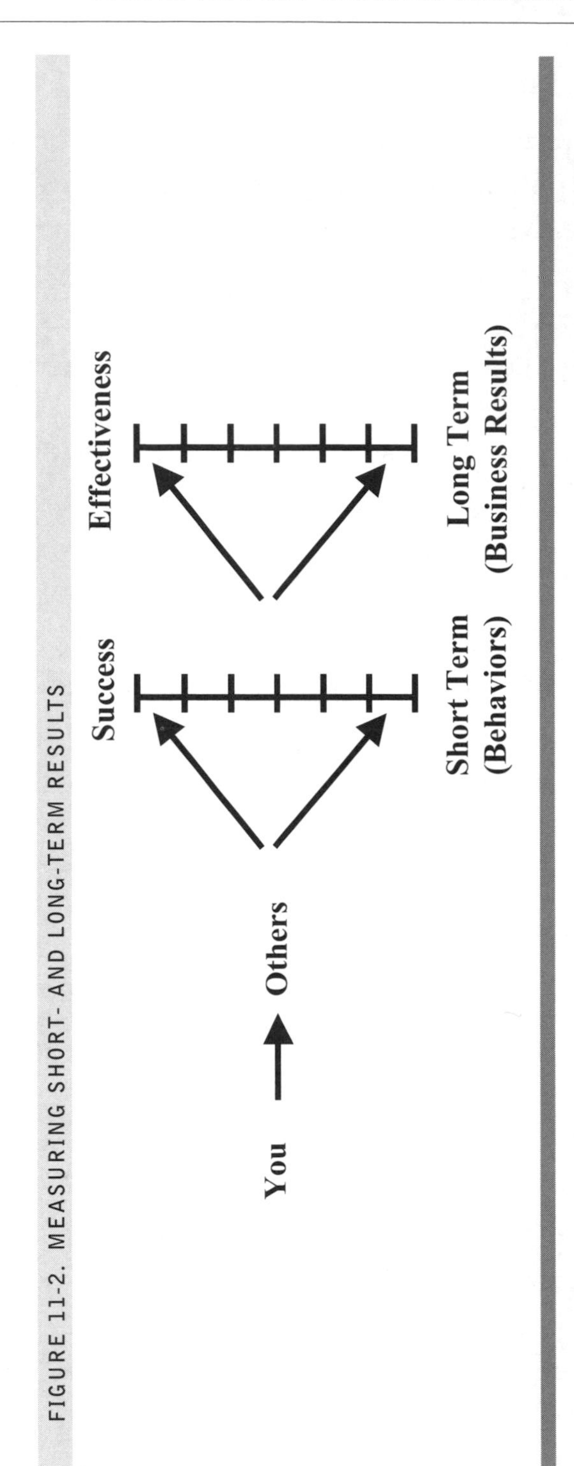

FIGURE 11-2. MEASURING SHORT- AND LONG-TERM RESULTS

intervention. Though you may have successfully changed employee behavior, you need to evaluate whether this change has also positively impacted business results. Remember, performance is both the activity and the results.

This is much more than an academic exercise. Managers need evaluations in order to make decisions. Level 3 evaluations ensure that the investment in training or other performance-improvement interventions has changed the behavior of the employees. Level 4 evaluations determine the value of the training or other intervention—in other words, was there a positive return on investment, or "Was the pain worth the gain?"

There are many other reasons you should evaluate training and other performance-improvement initiatives. These include:

- Improving the quality of the training or other intervention
- Identifying the best performance-improvement strategies
- Identifying what else needs to be done to improve performance

You identified the measures you will use to determine your success and effectiveness when you started the project, determining the performance gap and setting the reasonable goal. When you described these in measurable terms, you included measures of success and effectiveness. Whenever possible, use existing measures of performance. For example, for sales performance, use actual sales data. For manufacturing, use existing measures for quantity, quality, time, and cost. For customer service, use measures of customer satisfaction, customer retention, and referrals. Using existing measures gives you a strong baseline as to the present level of performance and any change that results from the intervention. Senior management is more likely to see the impact of the intervention when you present changes in the numbers that they routinely use to track performance.

A Level 3 Evaluation

In 1983, the Coast Guard Training Center in Petaluma, California, trained about 4,000 students in twenty-five courses, none of which had ever been systematically evaluated. While course content was periodically rewritten, no feedback was ever obtained from the field to assess the effectiveness of the training. A more systematic approach was necessary, and the best tool was evaluation.[5]

After the curriculum was rewritten to correspond with desired behavioral outcomes for each course, surveys were sent to recent graduates and their supervisors. The intent was to assess (1) how well the graduates were able to adopt the desired behaviors, (2) how often those behaviors were evidenced on the job, and (3) how important it was that graduates be able to adopt those behaviors. Open-ended questions were also asked of supervisors to determine what else the graduates should have learned during the training that would have prepared them for their roles in the field.

This systematic assessment led to a continuous refinement of the courses, making the training more efficiently delivered and more relevant by removing material of little value and adding needed topics. The time students spent in class was reduced as job aids were introduced. The net savings to the Coast Guard was $3 million a year recurring from a base cost of $9 million for student and instructor salaries alone.

There are some critics who feel that self-reports are not reliable enough for Level 3 evaluations. While I agree that direct observation is a better Level 3 technique, it is not always feasible. Coast Guard graduates are dispersed around the world upon completion of training. The self-report feedback is the next best thing, obtained for a fraction of the cost of other measurement methods. It is an example of the old 80/20 rule in action: for 20 percent of the cost, the Coast Guard gets 80 percent of the information needed.

A Level 4 Evaluation

In 1995, Century 21 Real Estate Corporation redesigned the one-week training program it provides to over 15,000 to 20,000 new real estate agents each year, offered by more than 100 trainers in various locations. A pre- and post-test system (Level 2 evaluation) was added to the participant evaluation (Level 1 evaluation) that had been used in the previous version of the course.[6] In addition, to measure the effectiveness of the training, the graduates' progress was tracked through a sales-performance system (Level 4 evaluation). That is, the number of sales, listings, and commissions for each graduate was cross-referenced to the office where they worked and the instructor who delivered the training.

While the initial goal of the evaluation was to measure the value of the training, the more important return was in being able to provide feedback regarding the actual performance of the graduates and to improve the performance of the sales managers and instructors. Before this Level 4 evaluation, instructors were rated primarily on feedback from the participant evaluations. By tracking the students' performance post-graduation, there was a better measure of instructor performance.

For example, when the graduates were tracked by office, different patterns of success were observed. A typical class had eighteen to twenty-four new agents from various offices in the same geographic area. In reviewing agents' performance during the six months that followed training, managers found unusual patterns of success. For instance, several agents from the same office greatly outperformed agents from another office who had taken the same course with the same instructor at the same time. It soon became obvious that agents from some offices had a higher probability of success than those from other offices. Graduates were then surveyed to identify the differences in work environments that contributed to varying performance. Not surprisingly, the high-performing graduates came from offices where they received direction, had access to ongoing training, and received psychological support. The low-performing graduates tended to be from offices where all or some of these factors were not present.

Subsequently, the titles of the more than 100 trainers were changed to Sales Performance Consultant. While still responsible for delivering the training, they now worked with the field offices to better shape the environments to which the graduates would return. About 120 business consultants were also given access to the performance data so as to provide feedback to the brokers regarding the work environment of their offices and the impact it was having on their new salespeople.

Another lesson learned concerned overreliance of Level 1 evaluations to assess the instructors' performance. In one case, a trainer rated in the bottom third of all trainers by his students was found to be one of the most effective when the first three months' performance of his graduates was examined. Why? During the course, the trainer was running evening sessions that gave the students an immediate opportunity to practice what they had just learned. After hearing about how to make cold calls to identify potential clients, the graduates would spend two hours that evening making such calls and another hour debriefing what they had done. Some of them made appointments to meet those prospects whom they contacted during the evening sessions during their training. While they were unhappy about working evenings (as was reflected in the Level 1 evaluations), they were being much better prepared for the working world.

Level 3 and Level 4 Evaluations as Part of the Intervention

Sometimes it is easier to sell the idea of more in-depth evaluations as an integral part of the intervention rather than as a separate event. As was mentioned in Chapter 6, the act of measurement encourages graduates of training programs to use what they have learned in the classroom. While many organizations view evaluation as "nice to have" at best, managers need to show that evaluations can be an important part of the overall intervention strategy.

The very act of measuring performance encourages the use of what has been learned in the training and reinforces desired changes that are associated with other performance-improvement initiatives. This may be an application of the Hawthorne Effect (the tendency of individuals and groups to perform better if they believe they are being observed), in that the act of evaluation is a form of observation that leads to increased performance.[7] By tracking individual and collective performance after training, a manager encourages use of what was learned in the classroom while obtaining information that can be used to provide feedback to employees so they can improve their performance. In tracking the progress in converting leads into actual sales, and then evaluating this progress, salespeople become more motivated to follow up leads that might otherwise have lapsed.

Tips on Evaluating the Results of Performance-Improvement Initiatives

Use the following tips to compile more in-depth evaluations of your performance-improvement interventions.

- Evaluation should focus on intermediate goals (improving quality, customer service, and cost reduction) as well as desired business outcomes (sales, profitability, and market share).
- Use existing measurement systems where possible. Since they already exist, there is baseline information available, management believes the metrics measure a desired business outcome, and it's cheaper than setting up a new evaluation system.
- Evaluation should be used as part of the intervention itself. The act of measuring encourages the use of what was learned. Evaluation improves transference.
- Use multiple measures so that performance is not driven by just one desired outcome.
- Evaluation documents the improvement as your people move from their present level of performance toward the desired level of performance.
- The work environment can be more important than the classroom experience in determining what gets transferred back to the job.

APPLICATION EXERCISE

Use Figure 11-3 to evaluate the ongoing analysis you have been developing for your workgroup. (For a larger version of this and the other application exercise forms, visit www.aboutiwp.com.)

FIGURE 11-3. WORKSHEET FOR EVALUATION-OF-CHANGE EXERCISE

How will you evaluate the short-term success of the training your people receive or any interventions you make as a manager?

How will you evaluate the long-term success of the training your people receive or any interventions you make as a manager?

List the business metrics your organization uses to measure results.

How are you going to link the results your workgroup gets with what your organization already measures?

Notes

1. Brenda Sugrue, *Annual Report of the Industry* (Alexandria, VA: ASTD, 2005).
2. Donald L. Kirkpatrick, *Evaluating Training Programs*, 2nd ed. (San Francisco, Berrett-Koehler, 1998).
3. Roger D. Chevalier, "Evaluation: The Link between Learning and Performance," *Performance Improvement* 43, no. 4 (April 2004): 40–44.
4. Brenda Sugrue, *Annual Report of the Industry* (Alexandria, VA: ASTD, 2005).
5. Roger D. Chevalier, "Systematic Change," *Performance and Instruction*, 29, no. 5 (May/June 1990): 21–23.
6. Jeanne Strayer and Roger D. Chevalier, "From Training to Performance," in *Performance Technology 1995* (Washington, DC: International Society for Performance Improvement, 1995), 55–57.
7. Fritz J. Roethlisberger, *Management and Morale* (Boston: Harvard University Press, 1941).

"Change agents either come with thick skin or develop a lot of scar tissue."

—ROGER CHEVALIER

CHAPTER 12

The Manager as Change Agent: A Case Study

This chapter is a case study based on personal experience and involving a six-year process to change the culture and performance of a major training center.[1] The program was born during a meeting with my future boss in a hotel bar. Over a couple of drinks, we mapped out our strategy for change at the Coast Guard Training Center in Petaluma, California. Little did we know the impact of our plan, which would ultimately influence the way the Coast Guard trains its people.

I had worked with Captain Dick Marcott before, when I was in charge of the leadership and management school on the West Coast and he was in charge of the entire Coast Guard leadership program. He was assigned to become the commanding officer of the Coast Guard's west coast training center, and I was assigned to be in charge of the training division. Captain Marcott had insight into the culture of Training Center Petaluma because he was about to leave his present assignment as the head of the Coast Guard's training and education division, where he oversaw the operations of all of the Coast Guard's training centers. I also had some insight into Training Center Petaluma as that was where I had headed to leadership and management school four years before.

We started planning our strategy for change by sketching the change model described in Chapter 10. At first I thought he would play the role of the directive change agent and I would get to be the participative change agent. Then he told me that I would be the directive change agent and that he would be there to cover my back. Thus, we would need to find other staff members to play the participative change roles.

We knew that we did not have a complete picture of the situation but we could identify some of the performance gaps. In general terms, we knew that the efficiency and effectiveness of the training were not acceptable. My role initially was to get a clearer picture of these performance gaps and uncover the driving and restraining forces that shaped the center's present level of performance.

Captain Marcott then told me to call one of his staff officers and get a set of orders to spend one day at the Coast Guard Training Center on Governors Island in New York City, one day at the Coast Guard Training Center in Yorktown, Virginia, and two days with Charlie Swaringen. I asked who Charlie Swaringen was and was told I'd find out shortly. It turned out that Charlie was a civilian education specialist at the Coast Guard Training Center in Elizabeth City, North Carolina, and that the center there was the most advanced at using a systematic approach to training design and development. Charlie was one of the giants upon whose shoulders I would stand.

The Overall Situation

The training division at Petaluma consisted of 115 instructors, instructional designers, and support personnel who were responsible for assessing the need for training and then designing, delivering, implementing, and evaluating twenty-five courses delivered to 4,000 students a year. My responsibility was to create and implement a new mission, vision, and culture that would make the training more efficient and effective, as measured by reduced training costs and by improved performance of the graduates when they return to the field.

After arriving, I discussed present and desired levels of performance with key staff and observed performance at the training center; I used a lot of "management by wandering around" to accomplish this. I then met with key members of my staff, first individually and then as a group, to gain their input on uncovering the driving and restraining forces that influenced performance.

Present performance left a lot to be desired. There were performance gaps in the way the need for training was assessed, the way it was designed and developed, the way it was delivered in the classrooms, and the way it was evaluated. While the staff appeared to be working hard, they were not doing the right things.

Many restraining forces would have to be eliminated or weakened if performance was to improve. There was a lack of clear expectations, feedback, and performance coaching at all levels. There were no clearly defined processes and procedures for analysis, design, development, and evaluation. There was a lack of necessary equipment, with only two obsolete computers for the entire division. The evaluation and reward systems were not measuring and rewarding the right behaviors. Instructors and staff were not being properly selected, based on their motives, capacity, knowledge, and skills. The Performance Analysis Worksheet showing the performance gaps and the driving and restraining forces is displayed as Figure 12-1.

Rationale for the Analysis and Changes Made

The following comments will explain why the Performance Analysis Worksheet factors were placed and weighted as shown in Figure 12-1. Both analyses and subsequent solutions are given beginning on page 174.

(text continued on page 174)

FIGURE 12-1. PERFORMANCE ANALYSIS WORKSHEET FOR CASE STUDY

Present Level of Performance: A training division staff that was working hard but was neither efficient nor effective in the way it developed and delivered training.

Desired Level of Performance: A nationally recognized training organization that uses systematic assessment and continuous improvement to deliver training efficiently and effectively.

Reasonable Goal: Have a systematic approach for the assessment, design, development, implementation, and evaluation of training in place within one year.

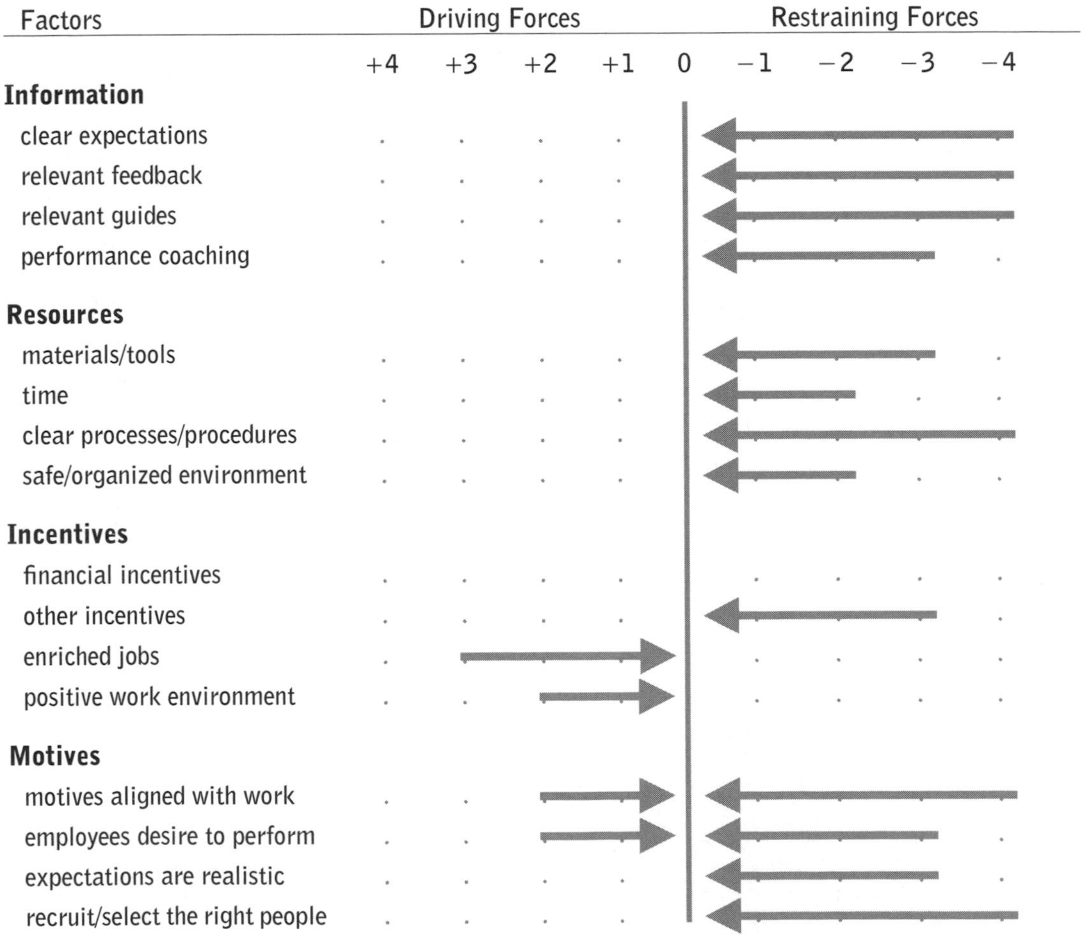

Factors	Driving Forces					Restraining Forces			
	+4	+3	+2	+1	0	−1	−2	−3	−4
Information									
clear expectations									
relevant feedback									
relevant guides									
performance coaching									
Resources									
materials/tools									
time									
clear processes/procedures									
safe/organized environment									
Incentives									
financial incentives									
other incentives									
enriched jobs									
positive work environment									
Motives									
motives aligned with work									
employees desire to perform									
expectations are realistic									
recruit/select the right people									

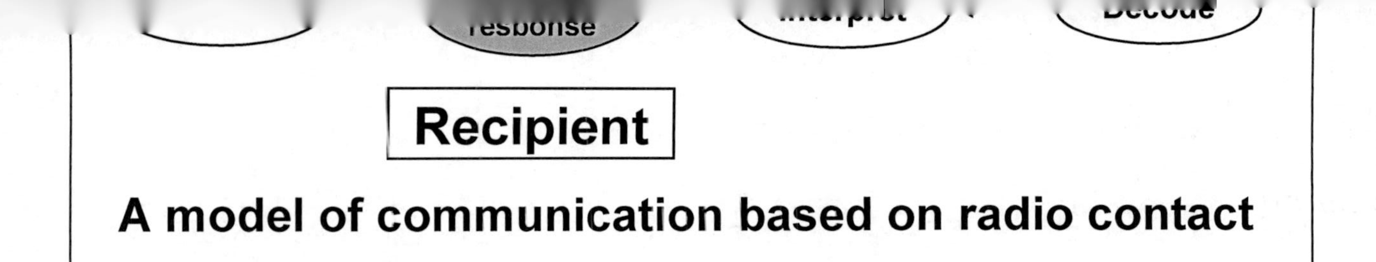

A model of communication based on radio contact

European - American

↓ at maturity

↓ at any point until maturity

European call option maturity

at fine T, stock price X and

price of underlying asset of maturity

S_T (price now S_0)

option premium (price) → c

At maturity (T) buyer (longcall) has to decide, and the decision will depend on the price at maturity

$S_T > X$ → buy the asset, because I will buy something at X, and the market price S_T

$S_T - X - c$ = will be the profit or loss

$S_T \leq X$ => don't buy it because its not worth it.

X => stock price

profit / loss

long call

S_T

X

$-c$

zero profit
↳ $S_T = X + c$

For prices lower than X => the writer keeps the premium

For prices higher than X

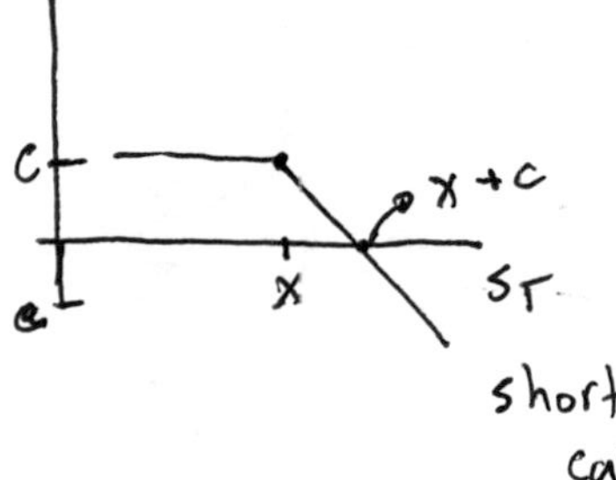

COMMUNICATIONS

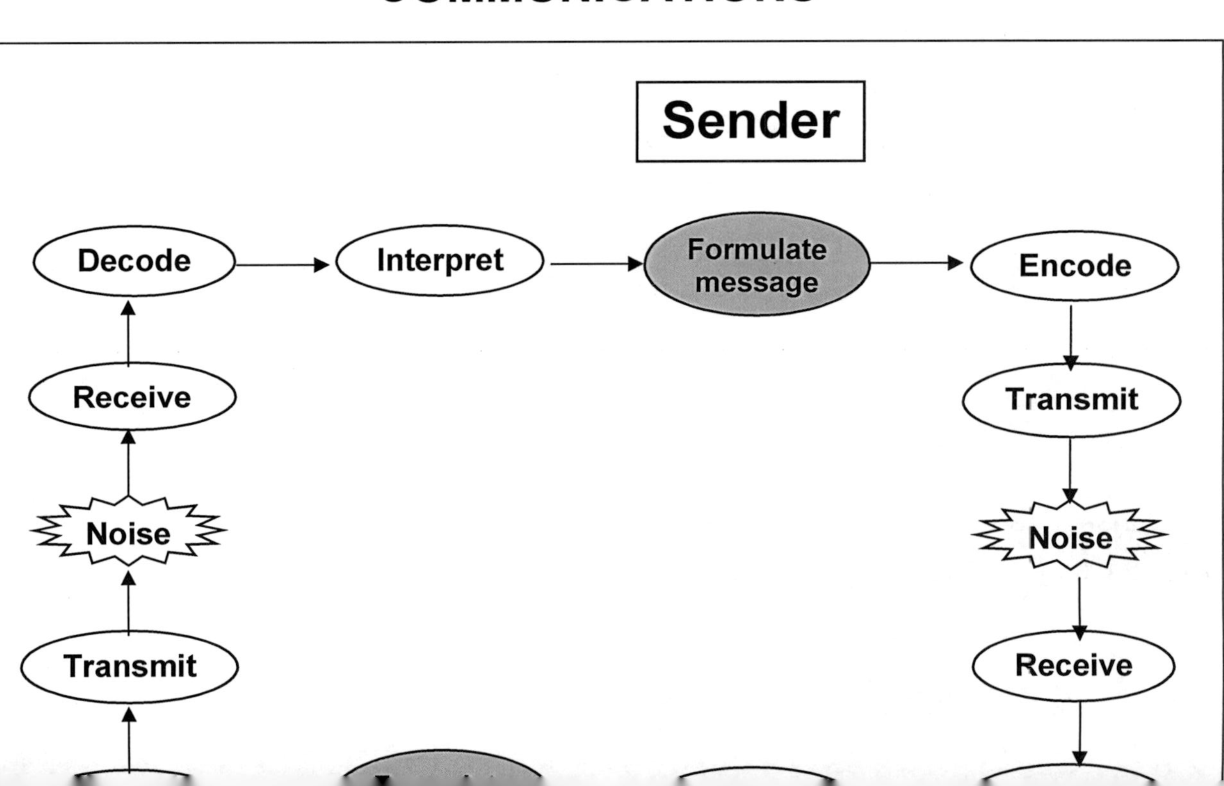

Factors	Driving Forces (+4 +3 +2 +1)	Restraining Forces (−1 −2 −3 −4)
Capacity		
capacity to learn	+2	
capacity to do what is needed	+2	
recruit/select the right people	+2	−3
emotional limitations	+2	−2
Knowledge/Skills		
required knowledge		−3
required skills		−4
placement		−2
cross-trained		−2

Factors	Driving Forces					Restraining Forces			
	+4	+3	+2	+1	0	−1	−2	−3	−4

Information

clear expectations

Analysis: Expectations of individual and group performance for all levels of personnel were not aligned with what was needed to be done to close the performance gap. *Solution:* Meetings were held with managers and staff to make sure that all personnel were aware of the new standards for performance.

relevant feedback

Analysis: Feedback at all levels was reinforcing the present level of performance. *Solution:* Once expectations were made clear, feedback was regularly given to individuals and groups on their willingness to change and their progress in doing so.

relevant guides

Analysis: Guides for the analysis, design, development, implementation, and evaluation of training either did not exist, were not used, or were not aligned with what was needed to improve performance. *Solution:* Guides were developed to assist staff members in their roles as course designers and as instructors.

performance coaching

Analysis: While some coaching was taking place, it focused on maintaining the present level of performance. *Solution:* A new performance-management system was developed that solicited employees' input on their own performance. This provided an opportunity for ongoing coaching and development.

Resources

materials/tools

Analysis: Much of the required equipment for designing and delivering training was either obsolete or nonexistent. *Solution:* New equipment was purchased, including computers to support course design and development of training materials.

time

Analysis: Most of the staff were working around 50 hours per week but were not doing the right things. More time would be necessary to make the needed changes. *Solution:* Nonproductive work was identified and reduced so that more time was available to make the needed changes. Key staff members were moved to positions that made them more responsive to doing what was needed to improve performance.

clear processes/procedures

Analysis: Processes and procedures for the analysis, design, development, implementation, and evaluation of training either did not exist, were not used, or were not aligned with what was needed to improve performance. *Solution:* Clearly defined processes and procedures for analyzing, designing, developing, delivering, and evaluating training were developed.

safe/organized environment

Analysis: While the work environment was safe, it was not properly organized, since there was no systematic approach to developing and delivering training. *Solution:* The division was reorganized

Factors | Driving Forces | Restraining Forces

+4 +3 +2 +1 0 −1 −2 −3 −4

to reflect the needed changes. While training was decentralized, those responsible for analysis, design, development, and evaluation reported to a centralized staff that ensured consistency of activities and results.

Incentives

financial incentives

Analysis: Financial incentives were not available in the military compensation system.

other incentives

Analysis: Medals and other awards were used infrequently and reinforced the wrong behaviors. *Solution:* Praise was given and medals awarded to those who made the most progress toward meeting the new standards.

enriched jobs

Analysis: The jobs of those who developed and delivered the training were very enriched, requiring a variety of skills and individual responsibility. *Solution:* New roles and responsibilities further enriched the number of skills and the amount of individual responsibility required.

positive work environment

Analysis: The work environment was positive, although it reinforced the wrong behaviors. *Solution:* This eventually led to a more positive work environment where personnel had greater opportunity to develop new skills.

Motives

motives aligned with work

Analysis: The course developers and instructors wanted to do the best job possible, although the mid-level managers were content to do "business as usual." *Solution:* The desire to change was rewarded while some mid-level managers had to be removed because they were seen as barriers to improving performance since they resisted the change effort.

employees desire to perform

Analysis: The staff wanted to do things right, but the mid-level managers wanted to maintain what was already being done. *Solution:* The new work environment encouraged a higher level of performance that was routinely rewarded.

expectations are realistic

Analysis: Expectations were aligned with the present level of performance, not the desired level of performance. *Solution:* While there were some doubts about the new standards, the staff met or exceeded all expectations.

recruit/select the right people

Analysis: Many members of the staff were assigned for reasons other than being the best people available to perform the roles needed to develop and deliver training. *Solution:* New standards for selection of instructors and managers were developed and used, resulting in better-qualified people who supported the change effort. All new personnel were handpicked using the same guidelines that included recent experience in what they would instruct, interpersonal skills, and a genuine concern for others.

Factors	Driving Forces					Restraining Forces			
	+4	+3	+2	+1	0	−1	−2	−3	−4

Capacity

capacity to learn

Analysis: Despite poor selection methods, many of the personnel had the capacity to learn what was needed to be successful. *Solution:* Better selection methods provided people with the capacity to learn and do what was needed to be successful.

capacity to do what is needed

Analysis: Despite poor selection methods, many of the personnel had the capacity to do what was needed to be successful. *Solution:* Better selection methods provided people with the capacity to learn and do what was needed to be successful.

recruit/select right people

Analysis: Some personnel were very qualified and would adapt to the new requirements, while others would not. *Solution:* All new personnel were selected to ensure that they had the necessary skills and attributes to be successful. Those who were not successful in the new environment were "selected out."

emotional limitations

Analysis: Most of the staff was willing to make the needed changes, although there was resistance from the mid-level managers. *Solution:* Six out of twelve mid-level managers were replaced during the first year by managers who were committed to the change effort.

Knowledge/Skills

required knowledge

Analysis: Personnel lacked the necessary knowledge to properly analyze, design, develop, implement, and evaluate training. *Solution:* With the staff being selected based on their experience, interpersonal skills, and caring about others, they responded well to the training provided to improve their ability to develop and implement training.

required skills

Analysis: Personnel lacked the necessary skills to properly analyze, design, develop, implement, and evaluate training. *Solution:* Following training, staff members were coached and developed in a positive work environment to develop the necessary skills to be successful.

placement

Analysis: Many personnel were not placed in roles that would capitalize on what they had to offer. *Solution:* Some staff members were better suited for analysis, design, development, and evaluation of training, while others were better suited for delivery of the training. Staff members were placed accordingly.

cross-trained

Analysis: There was no ongoing exchange of roles to ensure mutual understanding and support between those who delivered the training and those who developed it. *Solution:* Where possible, staff members were cross-trained to ensure that they understood how their roles impacted others.

Implementing the Change

My role in the process was to orchestrate the change in a way that corresponded with the way the training division did business. My most important job was to clearly communicate the change in expectations that would accompany a change in operations. In essence, I prepared the personnel for change. For example, I met everyone in the division at an "all hands" meeting that was held in the base theater at the close of a work day. I was presenting my vision of the future training center when I was asked, "Commander, if I understand you right, the students are now the most important people in the training division?"

I responded, "Chief, the students are not only the most important people in the division, they are the only reason we are here." I then added that instructors, who were previously considered to have the most important role in the division, had been moved down two notches because I had also elevated the course designers to the second position in this new pecking order.

Another example of how I communicated the new expectations was in the way I changed the performance-management system. The formal system had required that all personnel be evaluated in just three areas: proficiency, leadership, and conduct. In addition, evaluations under the old system were inflated, with most instructors receiving a perfect score, which made the system useless for improving performance. I added a new form to be completed by each division member before he would be evaluated every six months; the form included a brief description of the individual's role, a list of five accomplishments for the period, a list of five things he had done to develop professionally, and a list of three things he had done in the community to represent the Coast Guard in a good light. The purpose of the form was to communicate the new expectations and encourage acceptance of these standards by linking the descriptions to the performance appraisal.

The phrase that I embraced in my role of directive change agent was "Lead, follow, or get out of the way." I wanted people who were committed to the change and who would help lead the change. If I couldn't get commitment, I would accept compliance if they just went along with the change. If I couldn't get compliance, I would help them get another assignment so that I could select a better replacement.

In summary, I was responsible for communicating the overall vision; guiding the development of new training programs for the staff; developing the new performance-management system; implementing a structured way for the analysis, design, development, implementation, and evaluation of training; measuring outcomes; rewarding desired performance; and holding the staff accountable for shortfalls. While a directive change was necessary to communicate the new expectations and to overcome inertia, it would have a limited impact in the long term if it were not complemented with elements of participative change. To accomplish the participative change, I identified key informal leaders from the existing staff and brought in talented new personnel to assist. My job was to "turn up the heat," while theirs was to "put out the fires" by working with personnel who were willing to change.

A purely participative change strategy was considered but ruled out since it would not overcome the inertia, yield the systems needed for management and instructional design, or deal with those who would not accept the needed changes. However, I worked with key staff members to identify the important components of the change strategy. We first looked at elements of a participative-change strategy to identify ways to change the knowledge and skills of the staff. For instance, we brought in an outside consultant to present several different evening programs on adult learning theory and instructional design. We sent some of the staff to other organizations to benchmark what was being done. We implemented a new performance-management system to communicate expectations, encourage greater participation, and provide behaviorally specific feedback. We complemented these initiatives with a systematic evaluation of all training programs, measurements of results, and rewards for greater training efficiency and effectiveness. I also changed the performance-management and reward systems to reflect the new ways of doing business and new desired results. Members of my immediate staff played participative-change roles by training the staff, listening to their concerns, facilitating problem-solving groups, and gaining commitment from the staff.

As described in Chapter 11, the Level 3 evaluation of the change effort consisted of a survey sent to graduates and their supervisors. The goal was to determine the level at which graduates were able to perform, the frequency with which certain tasks were done, the importance of those tasks, and what else should have been taught. This provided the information we needed to eliminate extraneous material, add new topics, and identify potential job aids. The performance baseline allowed us to measure improvements in the preparation of students for the field as we reduced the time it took to train them. This also prepared personnel for further changes based on feedback from customers.

Based on the systematic assessment and continuous improvement process of a Level 3 evaluation, we were able to save our organization $3 million in recurring training expenses. Roughly $2 million was saved in student salaries by reducing training time, and another $1 million was saved in instructor salaries with reductions in staff. Because of the service nature of our organization, a Level 4 evaluation was too difficult and expensive to do. Nevertheless, the Level 3 evaluation provided information to make our training more efficient and effective. Other measures of success included feedback from our parent organization regarding the improved curriculum outlines, organizational awards for improved efficiency, and professional association awards for our performance-improvement efforts.

Results

The performance of the training center was so improved that it received two consecutive Unit Commendations from the Coast Guard for two-year periods ending in 1987 and 1989. In 1989, six years after the change process was begun, the training center was recognized by the Armed Forces Chapter of the National Society for Performance and Instruction (NSPI) as the Military Training Organization of the Year for 1988.

But the results went much further, influencing the entire Coast Guard training system. The methodologies for analysis, design, development, implementation, and evaluation were exported to the other Coast Guard training centers through a Performance Systems School that was developed to train instructors and designers from all the other training centers. The efforts made at the training center in Petaluma were part of a culture change that led to improved methodologies for training all Coast Guard personnel.

Tips on Being a Change Agent

- Be sure you have the support of your seniors and peers before implementing change.
- Analyze before you act; the most obvious solution usually treats a symptom rather than the underlying causes.
- Multiple solutions are necessary for complex problems.
- Create and communicate a clear vision of the desired future state.
- While the end (improved performance) is very often not negotiable, the means (how the change is done) usually is.
- Be prepared for resistance to change.
- Measure your results in terms that senior management will understand.
- Managers who successfully implement change might not win popularity contests but are invaluable to the continued success of their organizations.

Note

1. Roger Chevalier, "Systematic Change," *Performance and Instruction* 29, no. 5 (May/June 1990): 21–23.

SECTION 3

Synergy

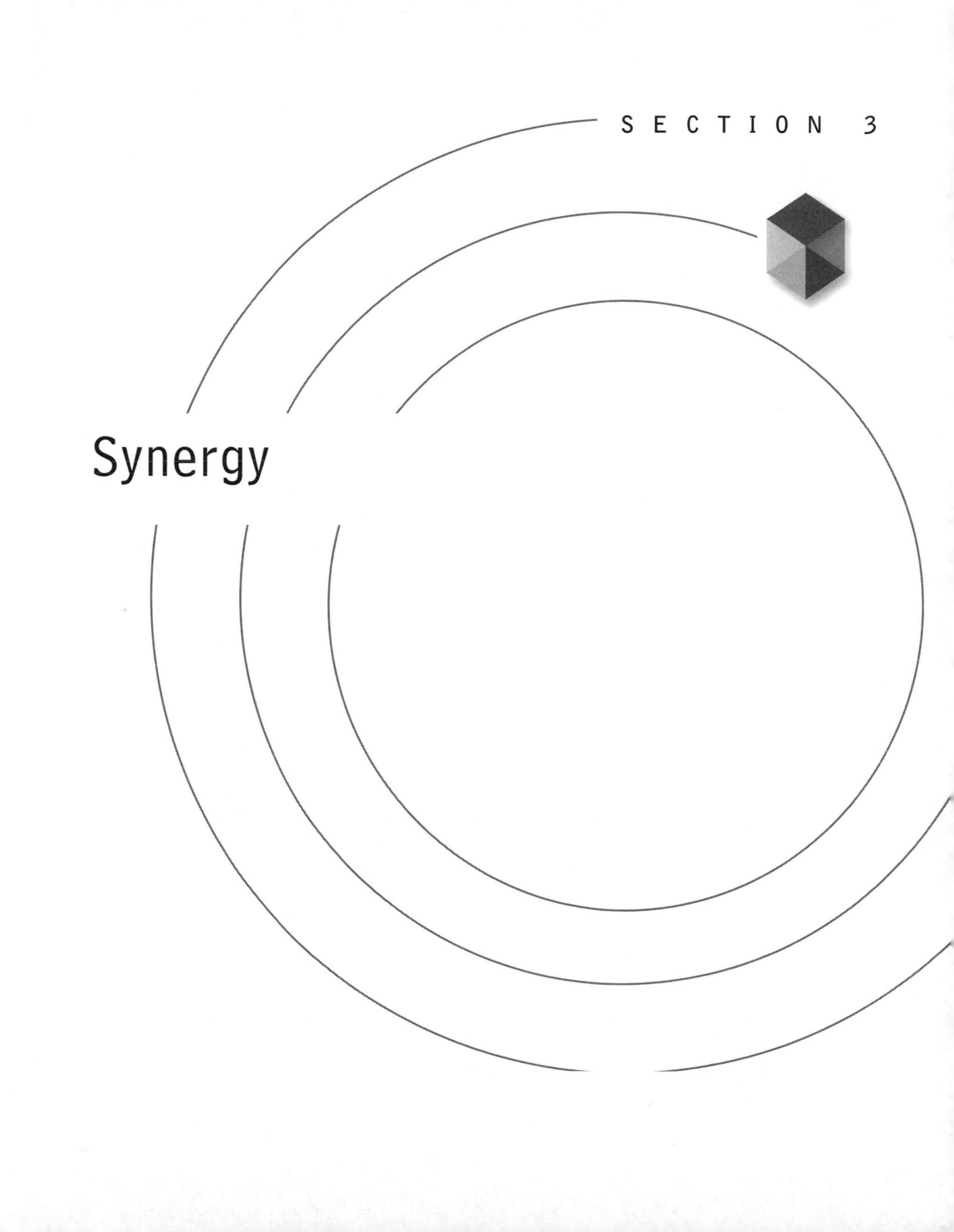

Synergy: when the whole is greater than the sum of the parts.

CHAPTER 13

Using All the Tools

This book has presented a number of tools for the management toolbox. While there is value in each tool individually, their real power is unleashed when used together. The whole really *is* greater than the sum of its parts. This chapter reviews the major tools and describes how to combine them. However, to realize their full value, you need to bring two important elements to the process: your work experience and your belief in developing people to their fullest potential.

Performance Coaching

The performance-coaching process, introduced in Chapter 1 and reproduced here in Figure 13-1, embraces what you need to do to develop your employees. Performance coaching complements nearly every performance-management and/or appraisal system; the process presented in this book provides a structure for the way you can interact with employees during the appraisal periods. As explained in Chapter 1, the process begins with planning, communicating expectations regarding ac-

FIGURE 13-1. THE PERFORMANCE-COACHING PROCESS.

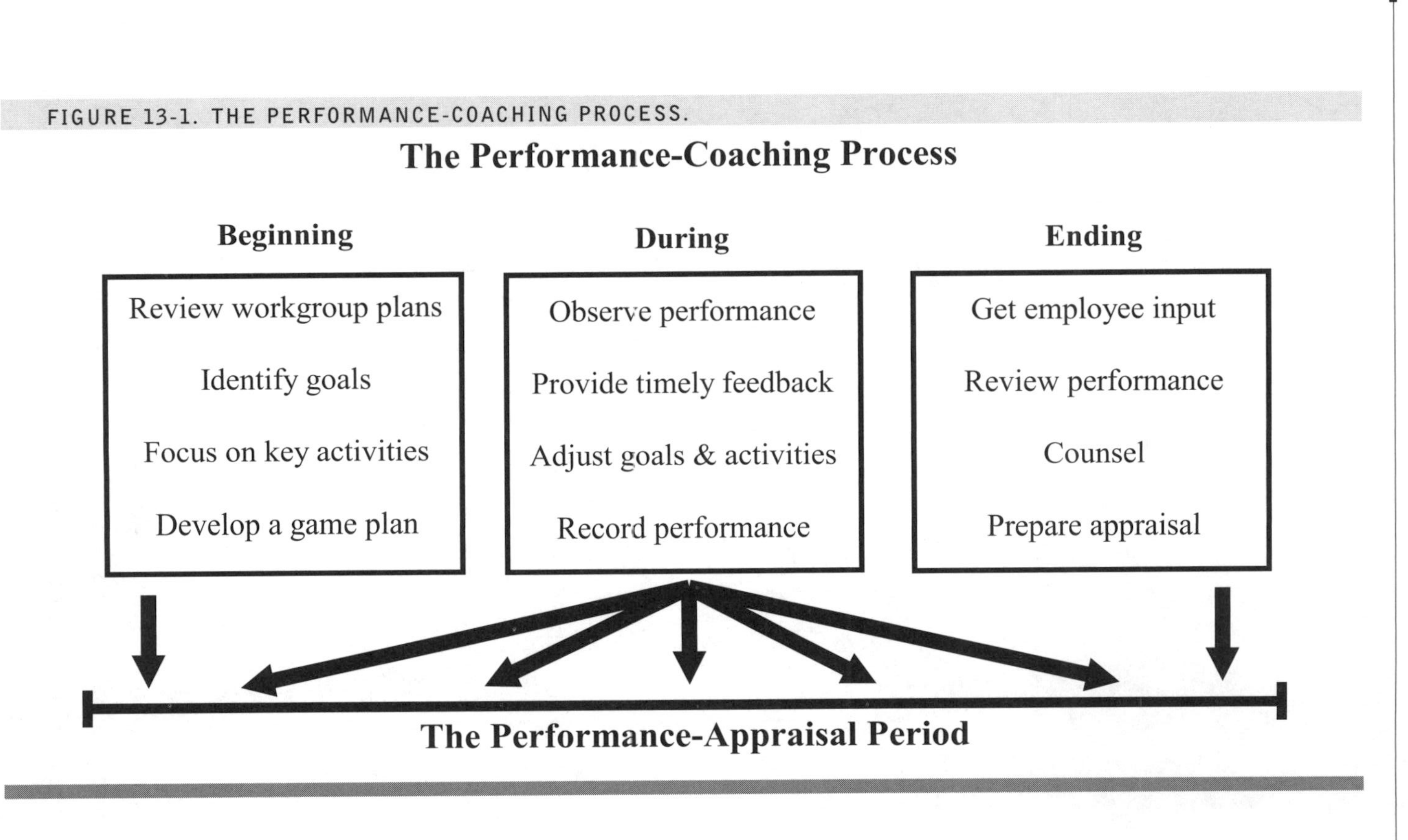

tivities and results, and developing a game plan for the appraisal period. During the entire period, you routinely observe the performance of your employees, provide timely and specific feedback, keep good records, and adjust the goals as necessary. The process ends with a counseling session that focuses on reinforcing positive performance and urging continued development of areas that fall short. The counseling session itself begins by soliciting input from your employees as to how they see their performance, and reviewing your records before counseling them and then writing your appraisals.

Situational Leadership

The Situational Leadership Model, as presented in Chapter 2 and reproduced here in Figure 13-2, is a structure for analyzing the readiness of your employees to do specific tasks based on their willingness and ability and then choosing the appropriate leadership style. You vary the amount of direction and support you give employees, based on their willingness and ability to do specific tasks during the performance-appraisal period.

When beginning the performance-coaching process, vary your leadership style based on the employee's readiness level. For low-readiness personnel, you will need to communicate your performance expectations clearly in order for the individuals to be successful. For high-readiness personnel, you can encourage the individuals to participate in the goal-setting process for those activities they need to do well to be successful. Similarly, you will observe and give feedback to low-readiness employees but provide feedback on goal accomplishment to high-readiness employees.

Performance Counseling

The Performance Counseling Guide, introduced in Chapter 3 and reproduced here in Figure 13-3, is based on the principles of Situational Leadership and describes how to lead employees in a formal counseling session. In essence, you back through the model from Style 4 to Style 3 to Style 2 (S4, S3, S2) as you assess the readiness

(text continued on page 188)

FIGURE 13-2. THE SITUATIONAL LEADERSHIP® MODEL

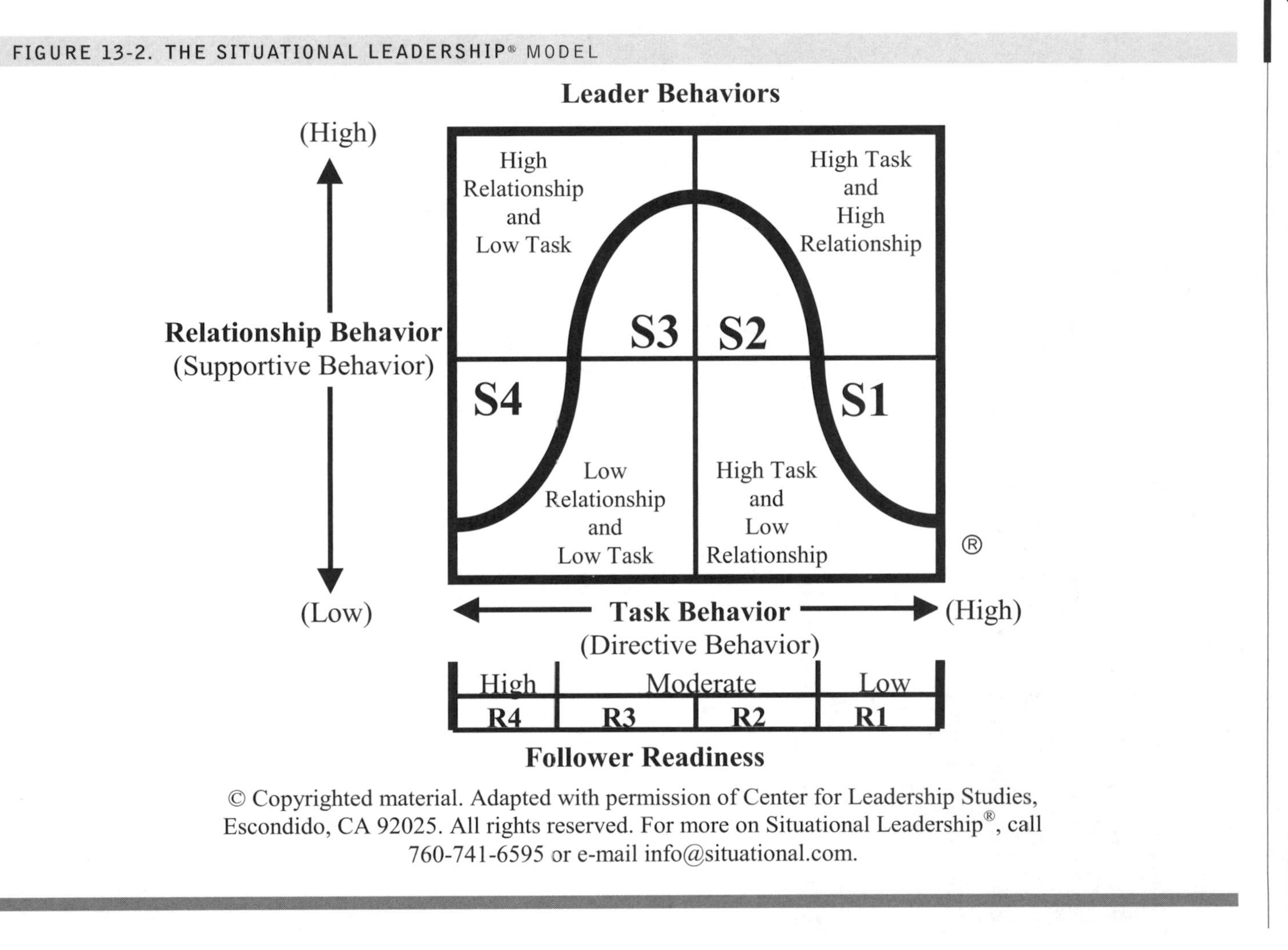

FIGURE 13-3. THE PERFORMANCE COUNSELING GUIDE SHOWING LEADERSHIP STYLE MATCHED TO FOLLOWER READINESS

Performance Counseling Guide

Assessment of Follower Readiness

S4: Prepare	S3: Assess	S2: Diagnose
Low Direction Low Support	Low Direction High Support	High Direction High Support
1. Observe, monitor, and track performance.	1. Build rapport, trust, and personal power.	1. Focus discussion with direct questions.
2. Review your records and employee input.	2. Begin session with open-ended questions.	2. Identify readiness level for each issue.
3. Set counseling goals and develop a strategy.	3. Identify issues and problem ownership.	3. Select an appropriate leadership style.

S4: Follow Up	S3: Reinforce	S2: Develop	S1: Prescribe
Low Direction Low Support	Low Direction High Support	High Direction High Support	High Direction Low Support
1. Document session in performance record.	1. Reinforce self-worth and self-esteem.	1. Discuss activities/goals to improve performance.	1. Clearly communicate expectations and goals.
2. Follow through on all commitments.	2. Assess understanding and commitment.	2. Reach agreement on best course of action.	2. Define role as both means and ends.
3. Observe, monitor, and track performance.	3. Encourage, support, motivate, and empower.	3. Guide, persuade, explain, and train.	3. Inform, describe, instruct, and direct.

Selection of Leader's Style Matched to Follower Readiness

Able & willing & confident	Able but unwilling or insecure	Unable but willing or confident	Unable & unwilling or insecure
R4	R3	R2	R1

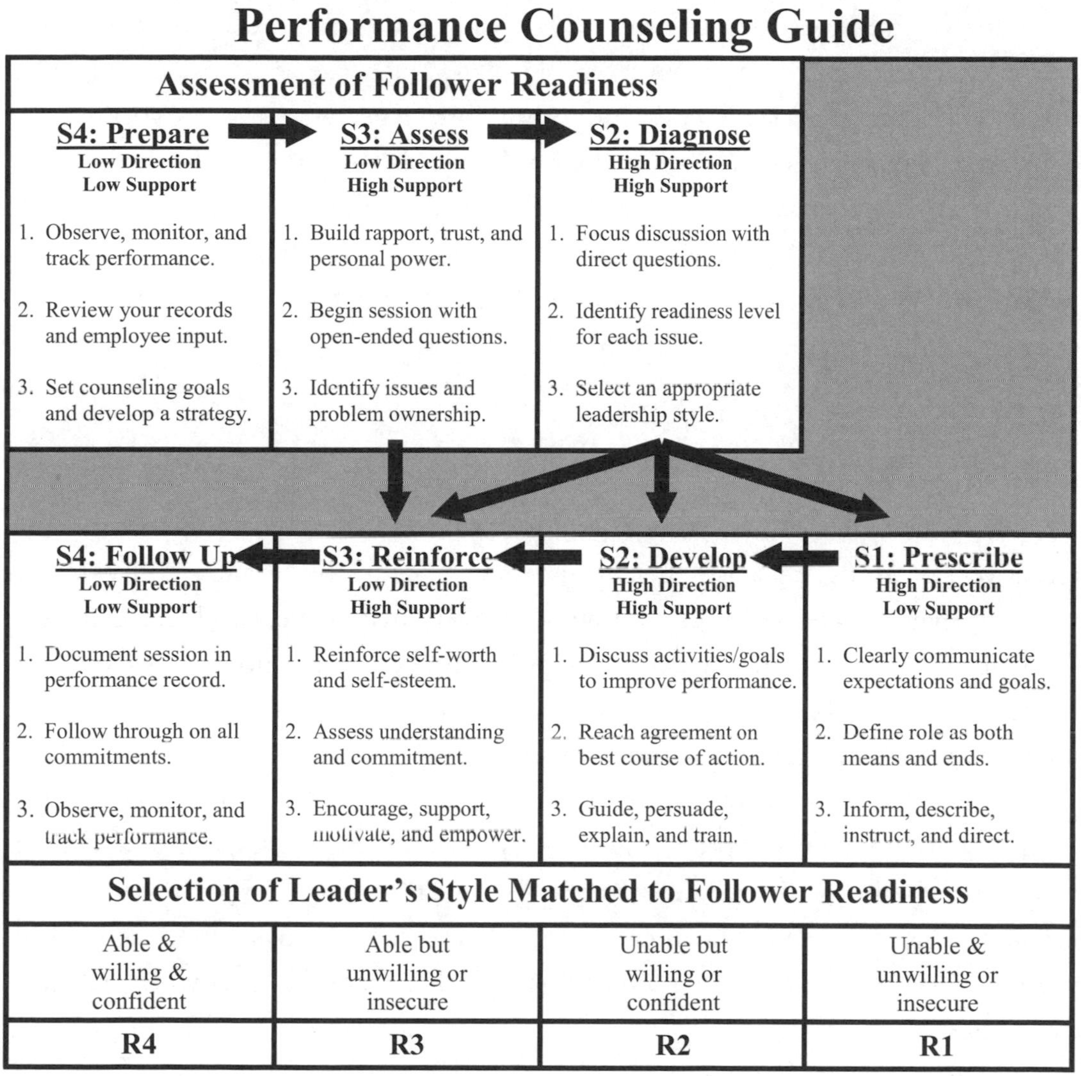

of your employees to do specific tasks. You also assess the location of problems in terms of how you and the employees see the situation.

After you've assessed your employees' readiness levels, you chose the appropriate leadership style for your intervention. You should use an S1, describing what needs to change and clearly communicating your expectations when you have an employee who is neither willing nor able to change, or does not see the performance problem at all. However, for an employee who sees the problem and is willing to change, S2 will do the job. S3 is used to provide feedback to an employee who is performing to standard but who lacks confidence. Lastly, S4 is for an employee who is truly willing and able to do the job.

Job Enrichment

Chapter 4 discussed employee needs and motivation. While it is good to know that employees do things to satisfy their own personal needs, the business application of this information is found in job enrichment. You satisfy lower-level needs for survival, security, and social interaction by providing acceptable policies, supervision, interpersonal relationships, salary, security, and low impact of the job on personal life before you can attempt any job enrichment.

Job enrichment is a way you can build opportunities for individuals to fulfill their higher-level needs by providing chances for achievement, responsibility, recognition, personal growth, and enjoyment of the work itself. You should review your employees' jobs to see how you can add to their personal satisfaction. Figure 13-4 presents a summary of the core dimensions of job enrichment that were presented in Chapter 4.

Building a High-Performance Team

There are a number of factors necessary to build a high-performance team. Selection in, training and development, and selection out all ensure that you have the right

FIGURE 13-4. JOB ENRICHMENT AS AN INTERVENTION

Job Enrichment

Task identity: Employees can identify with the final product and are not isolated from the results; employees produce an identifiable product that they can take pride in making.

Task significance: Employees can see how their work affects the finished product, the others they work with, and the customers who will use the product.

Variety of skills: Employees use many different skills to complete their work.

Autonomy: Employees make decisions regarding how the work process is done, such as the production schedule and procedures to do the job.

Feedback: Employees receive timely, specific feedback on the quality of their work.

Responsibility: Employees are given responsibility for the completion of the tasks.

employees in place. As a manager, you must also ensure that there is enough task behavior (direction) to keep the group focused, enough maintenance behavior (support) to keep the group together, and enough outlets for personal behavior.

You also should identify the informal groups, the informal leaders, and the unofficial norms for your workgroup. These need to align with the organization's culture, policies, and regulations. The greater the alignment of your workgroup and the organization, the more productive it will be. Figure 13-5, presented in Chapter 5 as Figure 5 1, describes this needed alignment.

Identifying Performance Shortfalls

Another important role you have as a manager is to identify performance shortfalls. One of the best ways to do this is to compare present and desired levels of performance in terms of quantity, quality, time, and cost. After setting these two endpoints, you identify a reasonable goal that lies between them and that can be accomplished in a relatively short time. Figure 13-6, introduced in Chapter 6, describes this process.

(text continued on page 192)

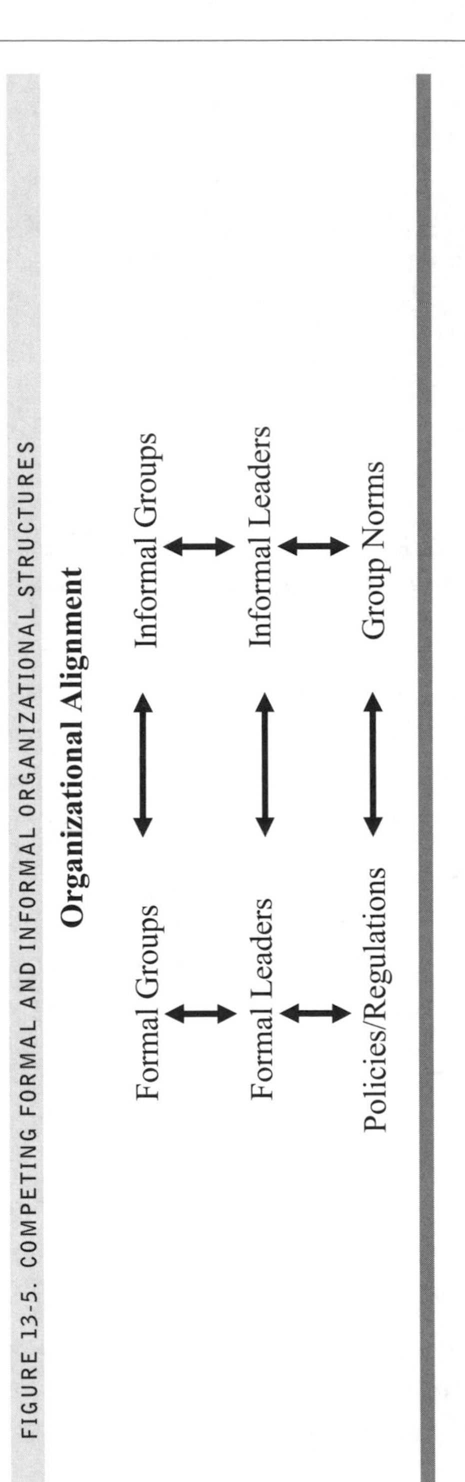

FIGURE 13-5. COMPETING FORMAL AND INFORMAL ORGANIZATIONAL STRUCTURES

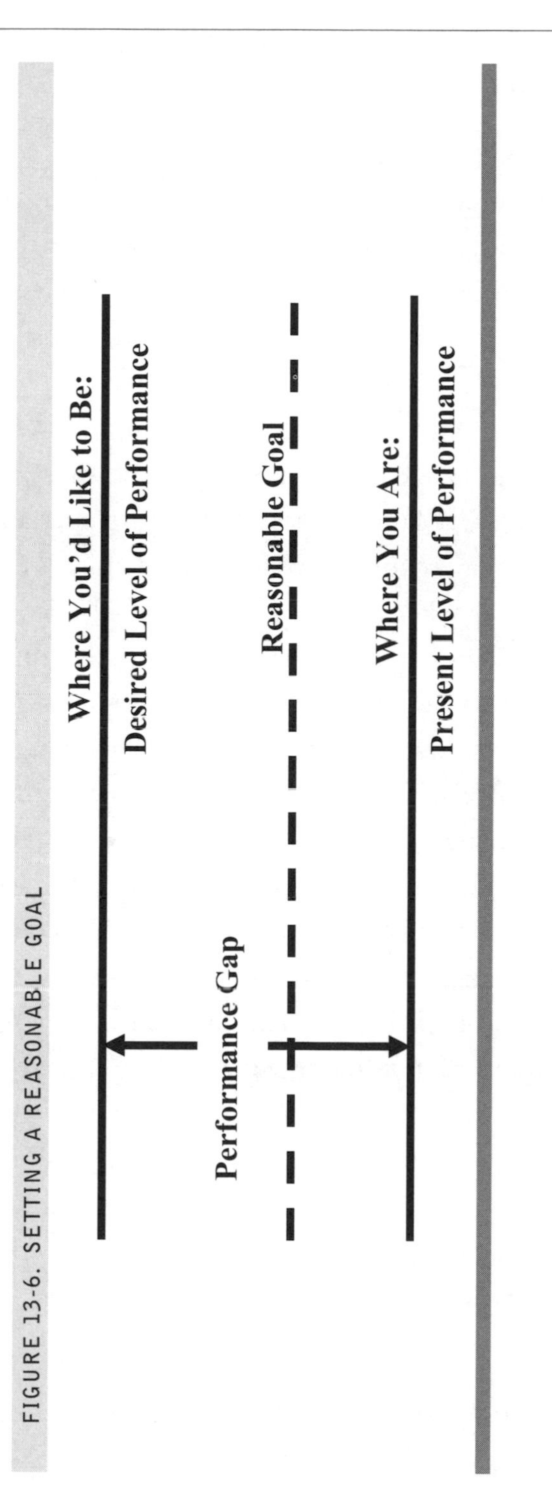

FIGURE 13-6. SETTING A REASONABLE GOAL

Analyzing the Causes

Once a performance gap has been described and the reasonable goal set, you then need to identify why performance is at its present level. All too often, a manager focuses on the employees as the cause of performance shortfalls, yet research has shown that about 85 percent of such shortfalls are the result of the work environment. For this reason, you begin your analysis by focusing on the work environment.

The work environment includes the information you provide as manager, the resources you make available to the employees, and the measurement and incentive systems that are in use. Many *information* factors overlap with the performance-coaching, leadership, and counseling tools already discussed, and they include clear expectations, timely feedback, relevant guides, and adequate coaching. *Resources* include time, equipment, materials, processes and procedures, and a safe work environment. *Measurement and incentives* include how performance is measured and rewarded, whether jobs are enriched, and how positive your employees find the overall work environment.

You must also look at your employees to see whether they are motivated, have the capacity to do and learn, and have the necessary knowledge and skills to be successful on the job. Employee motives must be aligned with what your organization can provide if individuals are to sustain positive performance. Employees should be selected for their motives and for their capacity to learn and do the job. Lastly, you need to examine whether your employees have the necessary knowledge and skills to do the job.

Do not think about developing solutions to close the performance gap before you have adequately identified its causes. In management, as in medicine, prescription without diagnosis is malpractice. Figure 13-7 here repeats Figure 7-5 and identifies the potential causes of performance gaps.

Performance Analysis Worksheet

The Performance Analysis Worksheet, depicted here as Figure 13-8, but introduced in Chapter 7 as Figure 7-7, is a way to systematically analyze and display the present

FIGURE 13-7. MODEL FOR ANALYZING POTENTIAL CAUSES OF PERFORMANCE GAPS

Cause Analysis Model

Work Environment

Information

1. Roles and performance expectations are clearly defined; employees are given relevant and frequent feedback about the adequacy of performance.
2. Clear and relevant guides are used to describe the work process.
3. Leadership and coaching guide employee performance and development.

Resources

1. Materials, tools, and time needed to do the job are present.
2. Processes and procedures are clearly defined and enhance individual performance if followed.
3. Overall physical and psychological work environment contributes to improved performance; work conditions are safe, clean, organized, and conducive to performance.

Incentives

1. Measurement and reward systems reinforce positive performance; financial and nonfinancial incentives are present.
2. Jobs are enriched to allow for fulfillment of employee needs.
3. Overall work environment is positive, where employees believe they have an opportunity to succeed; career-development opportunities are present.

Individual

Knowledge and Skills

1. Employees have the necessary knowledge, experience, and skills to do the desired behaviors.
2. Employees with the necessary knowledge, experience, and skills are properly placed to use and share what they know.
3. Employees are cross-trained to understand each other's roles.

Capacity

1. Employees have the capacity to learn and do what is needed to perform successfully.
2. Employees are recruited and selected to match the realities of the work situation.
3. Employees are free of emotional limitations that would interfere with their performance.

Motives

1. Motives of employees are aligned with the work and the work environment.
2. Employees desire to perform the required jobs.
3. Employees are recruited and selected to match the realities of the work situation.

FIGURE 13-8. BLANK PERFORMANCE ANALYSIS WORKSHEET

Present Level of Performance: ______________________________

____

Desired Level of Performance: ______________________________

____

Reasonable Goal: ______________________________

____

Factors	Driving Forces					Restraining Forces			
	+4	+3	+2	+1	0	−1	−2	−3	−4
Information									
clear expectations	.	.	.	.		.	.	.	.
relevant feedback	.	.	.	.		.	.	.	.
relevant guides	.	.	.	.		.	.	.	.
performance coaching	.	.	.	.		.	.	.	.
Resources									
materials/tools	.	.	.	.		.	.	.	.
time	.	.	.	.		.	.	.	.
clear processes/procedures	.	.	.	.		.	.	.	.
safe/organized environment	.	.	.	.		.	.	.	.
Incentives									
financial incentives	.	.	.	.		.	.	.	.
other incentives	.	.	.	.		.	.	.	.
enriched jobs	.	.	.	.		.	.	.	.
positive work environment	.	.	.	.		.	.	.	.
Motives									
motives aligned with work	.	.	.	.		.	.	.	.
employees desire to perform	.	.	.	.		.	.	.	.
expectations are realistic	.	.	.	.		.	.	.	.
recruit/select the right people	.	.	.	.		.	.	.	.

Factors	Driving Forces					Restraining Forces			
	+4	+3	+2	+1	0	−1	−2	−3	−4
Capacity									
capacity to learn	.	.	.	.		.	.	.	.
capacity to do what is needed	.	.	.	.		.	.	.	.
recruit/select the right people	.	.	.	.		.	.	.	.
emotional limitations	.	.	.	.		.	.	.	.
Knowledge/Skills									
required knowledge	.	.	.	.		.	.	.	.
required skills	.	.	.	.		.	.	.	.
placement	.	.	.	.		.	.	.	.
cross-trained	.	.	.	.		.	.	.	.

and desired levels of performance, to set the reasonable goal, and to identify the impact of the driving and restraining forces on closing the performance gap. Driving forces have different strengths, which you evaluate from a low of +1 to a high of +4. Restraining forces also have different strengths, which you evaluate from a low of −1 to a high of −4.

The completed Performance Analysis Worksheet gives you a snapshot of the performance gap and its causes. From that, you identify the factors that you have the ability to change and others that are out of your control. For a complex problem, it is not unusual to have many possible factors that you must change in order to improve performance.

Selecting the Solutions

Once you have determined the factors working for and against you, in order to close the performance gap, you select the best combination of solutions. As shown in Figure 13-9, and as originally introduced as Figure 9-2, you need to leverage the less expensive environmental factors (information, resources, and incentives) against the more expensive and usually less effective individual factors (motives, capacity,

FIGURE 13-9. LEVERAGING MULTIPLE PERFORMANCE SOLUTIONS

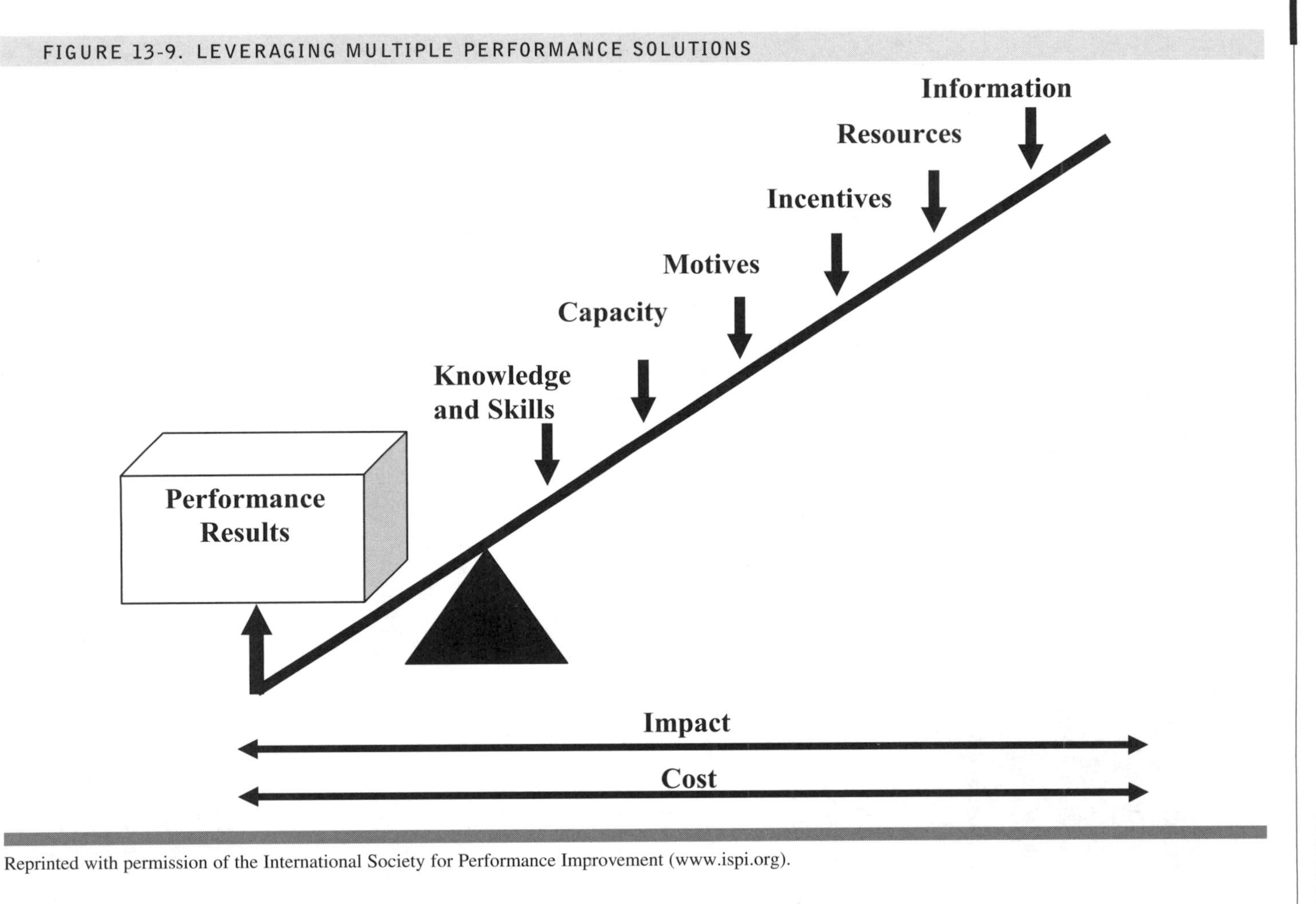

Reprinted with permission of the International Society for Performance Improvement (www.ispi.org).

and knowledge). Another application of this idea is to complement the training your employees will receive with clear expectations, feedback, and coaching, as well as to make sure that the necessary time, equipment, processes, and procedures are present and that the desired behaviors are measured and rewarded.

Implementing Change

It is necessary to take a balanced approach to implementing change. Participative change strategies, such as training and shared decision making, should be complemented with directive change strategies, such as consistent operating procedures and measurement systems. Figure 13-10, introduced originally as Figure 10-2, shows the relationship between participative and directive change. Participative change has great value in getting employees' commitment, but it can take a long time to have an effect. It requires that you have personal power with your people as they allow you to lead because of their respect for your personality, competence, and integrity. Directive change is quicker but might result in compliance only and might not have a lasting effect. It requires that you have position power with the authority to use rewards and sanctions for compliance. The best change strategies use aspects of both participative and directive change.

Evaluating Performance (Activities and Results)

Evaluation is necessary to encourage employees to do what they have learned and to evaluate the results of an intervention. Figure 13-11, introduced in Chapter 11 as Figure 11-1, organizes the types of interventions and the resulting activities and results. While many of the training interventions are controlled by others, you are still responsible for evaluating the results of the training and the other training and nontraining interventions you try. The training interventions that others provide should be evaluated using the the four levels described in Chapter 11.

As a manager, you have an investment in the training of your people. When they receive some form of classroom training, you have an opportunity cost for having them off the job to attend the training. When you train them on the job, your time

FIGURE 13-10. LEVELS OF CHANGE

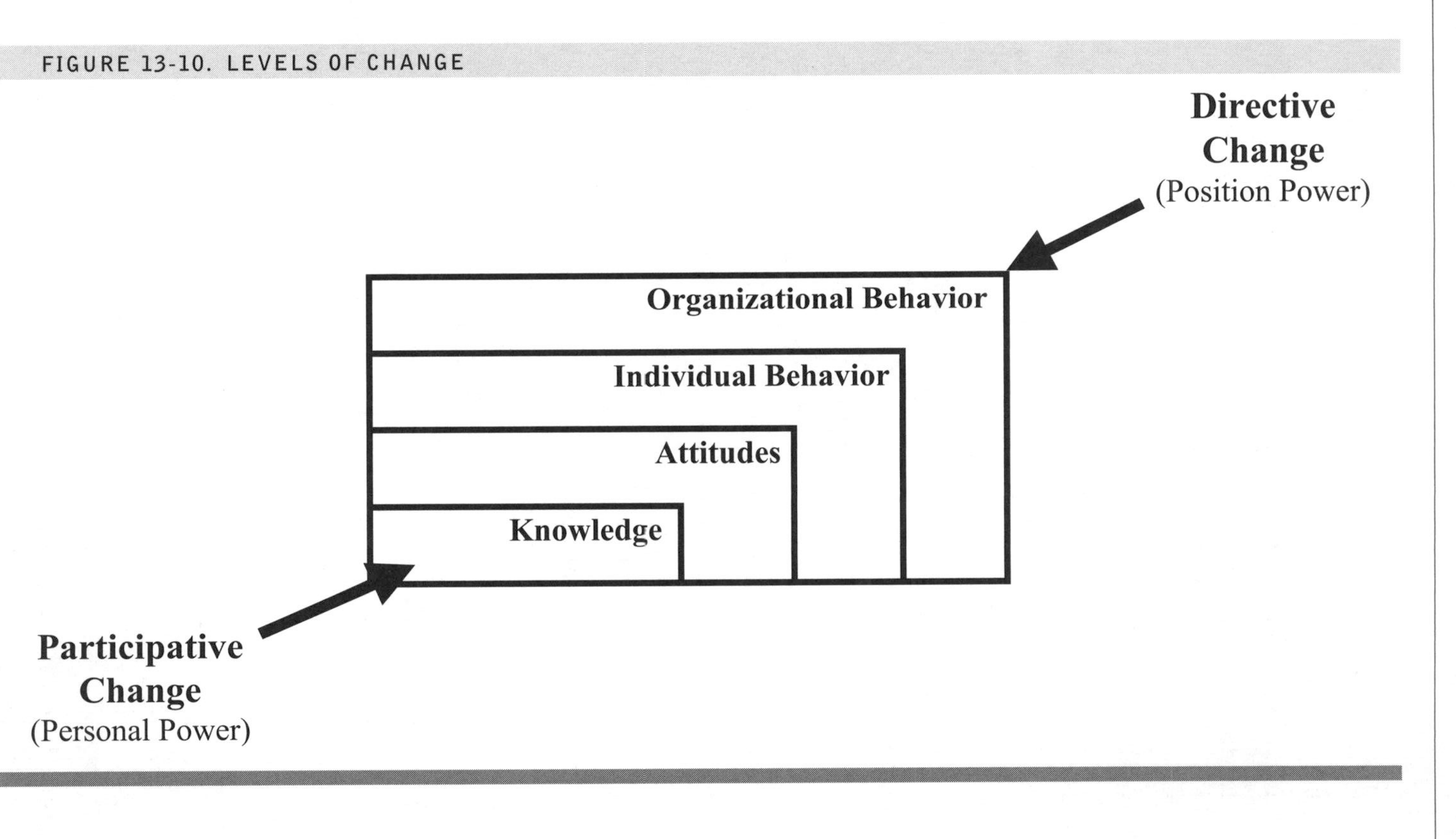

FIGURE 13-11. INTERVENTIONS, ACTIVITIES, AND RESULTS

Training Interventions	Nontraining Interventions	Activities	Results/Value
• Classroom • Simulator • Laboratory • Computer-Based Training (CBT) • Self-study • On-the-job training* • Mentoring* • Coaching* • Team building*	• Information* • Documentation* • Feedback* • Job aids* • Workplace design* • Organizational structure* • Empowerment* • Measurement* • Consequences* (rewards/sanctions)	Individual Behaviors and Organizational Behaviors • Work practices • Work processes Mitigating Factors • Leadership/coaching* • Measurement* • Incentives* • Tools/equipment* • Staffing* • Culture	• Quantity** • Quality** • Time** • Cost** • Productivity** • Sales** • Calls on warranty** • Customer retention** • Profitability** • Market share**
*Controlled by you	*Controlled by you	*Controlled by you	**Measured outputs

is another factor in the cost. With this investment you are making in training, you should be sure that your employees actually change the way in which they perform and that there is an actual return on investment as measured by increased productivity (quantity) and quality and/or decreased time and cost of production.

For your training and nontraining interventions, measure whether the behavior of your employees actually changes and whether the change increases productivity and quality, as well as decreases the time and cost of production.

Synergy in Conclusion

Never lose track of the fact that you create the work environment for your people. They will either excel or flounder based on the work environment you create with your coaching, leadership, counseling, and team-building skills, as well as the way in which you analyze performance gaps and causes, identify and implement solutions, and measure results. My hope is that you will use the tools presented in this book and will return to this book again and again as you see positive results each time.

Resources and Additional Reading

Internet Resources

For more information about the background to this book and to download full-size versions of the application exercises, visit the author's website at www.aboutiwp.com where you will find several articles that provide more in-depth material that served as the basis for this book.

For more information on Situational Leadership®, visit the Center for Leadership Studies at www.Situational.com.

For many exceptional free learning resources from Marshall Goldsmith, visit www.marshallgoldsmithlibrary.com.

For more information on performance improvement, visit www.ispi.org where you will learn more about the International Society for Performance Improvement. Also visit www.performancexpress.org for a free monthly newsletter with short articles on performance improvement.

For three great articles on organizational change, partnering, and leadership, visit www.vanguardc.com.

For more information on the relationship between training and performance, visit Harold D. Stolovitch & Associates at www.hsa-lps.com.

For more information on the role of training in performance improvement, visit the Center for Effective Performance at www.cepworldwide.com.

Books to Further Your Development in Leadership, Coaching, and Performance Improvement

Management of Organizational Behavior, Eighth Edition, Paul Hersey, Kenneth H. Blanchard, and Dewey E. Johnson (Upper Saddle River, N.J.: Prentice Hall, 2001). From the creators of Situational Leadership, one of the most successful management books ever written.

Handbook of Human Performance Technology, Third Edition, James A. Pershing, editor (San Francisco: Pfeiffer, 2006). A comprehensive collection of articles from some of the best performance improvement professionals.

Coaching for Leadership, Marshall Goldsmith, Laurence Lyons, and Alyssa Freas, editors (San Francisco: Jossey-Bass/Pfeiffer, 2000). A great collection of articles on leadership and coaching from a variety of authors.

Coaching for Leadership, Second Edition, Marshall Goldsmith and Laurence Lyons, editors (San Francisco: Pfeiffer, 2006). The second edition with many new authors and articles on leadership and coaching.

Training Ain't Performance, Harold D. Stolovitch and Erica J. Keeps (Alexandria, Va.: ASTD Press, 2004). An exceptional presentation of the relationship between training and performance.

Fundamentals of Performance Technology, Second Edition, Darlene M. Van Tiem, James L. Moseley, and Joan Conway Dessinger (Silver Spring, Md.: International Society for Performance Improvement, 2004). An excellent resource for those who want more information on the systematic and systemic approach used in improving performance.

Conquering Organizational Change, Pierre Mourier and Martin Smith (Atlanta, Ga.: CEP Press, 2001). A great resource for those interested in understanding the process of organizational change.

Evaluating Training Programs, Third Edition, Donald Kirkpatrick and James D. Kirkpatrick (San Francisco: Berrett-Koehler, 2005). The best book around on evaluation of training and other performance improvement interventions.

The Performance Appraisal Question and Answer Book, Dick Grote (New York: AMACOM, 2002). Addresses more than 140 commonly asked questions about the dreaded appraisal process, with straightforward, practical answers for managers and HR practitioners alike.

Coaching, Counseling & Mentoring, Second Edition, Florence M. Stone (New York: AMACOM, 2007). Distinguishes between three performance improvement techniques and when each is most appropriate.

The Nature of Leadership, B. Joseph White with Yaron Prywes (New York: AMACOM, 2007). A unique and exceptionally readable view of what it takes to be a great leader, including a survey to help you identify your strengths, preferences, and self-development needs.

Beyond Training and Development, Second Edition, William J. Rothwell (New York: AMACOM, 2005). A comprehensive, step-by-step guide to move "Training" from a concentration on quick fixes to become a driver of long-term, demonstrable human performance improvements across the organization.

Articles and Book Chapters by Roger Chevalier

The following articles and book chapters (some of which appear in the books listed above) will provide background information that served as the basis for this book:

"Leadership in Performance Consulting," *Handbook of Human Performance Technology*, Third Edition.

"Situational Leadership and Executive Coaching," with Paul Hersey, *Coaching for Leadership*, Second Edition.

Foreword to *Human Performance Technology Revisited*, Roger Chevalier, editor (Silver Spring, Md.: International Society for Performance Improvement, 2004).

"Evaluation: The Link Between Learning and Performance," *Performance Improvement,* vol. 43, no. 4 (April 2004), pp. 40–44.

"Updating the Behavioral Engineering Model," *Performance Improvement*, vol. 42, no. 4 (May/June 2003), pp. 8–13.

"Performance Consulting: Job Aids for Interacting with Clients," *Performance Improvement* vol. 40, no. 1 (January 2001), pp. 28–31.

"Situational Leadership and Performance Coaching," with Paul Hersey, *Coaching for Leadership.*

"HPT: The Power to Change," *Performance Improvement*, vol. 39, no. 1 (January 2000), pp. 23–25.

Index

About the Author

With more than 40 years of experience in management and performance improvement, Roger Chevalier is an independent consultant who specializes in integrating training into broader solutions. His past clients include a wide range of businesses, government agencies, and nonprofits. He has personally trained more than 30,000 managers, supervisors, and salespeople in performance improvement, leadership, coaching, change management, customer service, and sales programs in hundreds of workshops.

Major clients include Century 21 Real Estate Corporation, Sun Microsystems, State Farm Insurance, Johnson & Johnson, Hewlett Packard, Dell, Agilent Technologies, Medtronic AVE, E. &. J. Gallo Winery, Microsoft, Parker Hannifin, Siemens Energy and Automation, Phoenix Contact, Storage Dimensions, Energy Northwest, TRW, Vistakon, Realty World, Champion Chemicals, Borg Warner, World Learning, Nextel, the Department of Energy, the U.S Navy, the U.S. Coast Guard, NATO, and the International Atomic Energy Agency.

Roger is the former Director of Information and Certification for the International Society for Performance Improvement (ISPI). In this role, he was responsible for encouraging the use of performance technology with ISPI's 10,000 worldwide members by delivering presentations at professional conferences, instructing in ISPI's Institute public and in-house programs, establishing partnerships with other organizations, publishing articles, working with authors to publish their books, and certifying performance improvement professionals as Certified Performance Technologists (CPTs).

He is a former vice president of Century 21 Real Estate Corporation's Performance Division where he led a team of more than 200 consultants and trainers that developed and delivered sales and management programs for 80,000 sales associates in 5,000 offices nationwide. This role followed a sixteen-year relationship with Century 21 as a contract trainer and management consultant.

Roger is also a former U.S. Coast Guard commander whose final six-year tour was as training director for their west coast training center where he led 140 instructors and staff in implementing instructional systems design in 25 courses for 4,000 students a year. His training center was recognized by the National Society for Performance and Instruction (NSPI) as the "Military Training Organization of the Year" in 1989 for improving the quality of training while reducing recurring annual training costs by one third ($3,000,000 a year).

Roger is the author of numerous articles on human performance technology, leadership, coaching, management of change, customer service, and sales techniques published in a wide variety of professional and trade journals. He is a faculty member for ISPI's *Principles and Practices* program and has been a regular presenter at ISPI and ASTD annual conferences.

He earned a Doctor of Philosophy degree in Applied Behavioral Science and two Master of Science degrees in Personnel Management and Organizational Behavior. His previous education includes Masters and Bachelor of Arts degrees in English literature. Roger has been certified in the field of performance technology by the International Society for Performance Improvement.